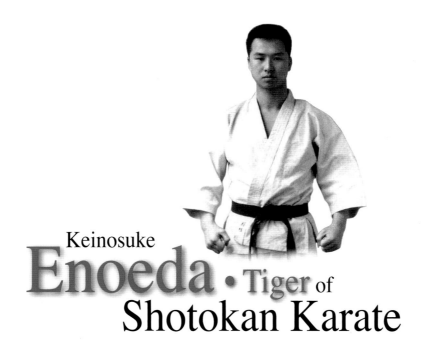

Keinosuke
Enoeda • Tiger of
Shotokan Karate

Keinosuke Enoeda – Tiger of Shotokan Karate

Published 2004 by Karate-London
PO Box 47428, London, N21 1TH, England
www.karate-london.co.uk

A catalogue record for this book is available from the British Library.
ISBN 0-9546947-1-6

Design and layout by Stephen Bere – Blue Island Publishing Ltd
22–24 Highbury Grove, London N5 2EA
info@blueIsland.co.uk
www.blueisland.co.uk

Printed and bound in Singapore by Craft Print PTE Ltd

Keinosuke Enoeda · Tiger of Shotokan Karate

by

Rod Butler

Acknowledgements

Mrs Reiko Enoeda
Ms Michie Enoeda
Mrs Chieko Buck
Sensei Yoshinobu Ohta (JKA England)
Sensei Hideo Tomita (JKA England)
Sensei Hideto Matsui
The Japan Karate Association, Tokyo
The Japan Karate Association, England
Stephen Bere – Blue Island Publishing
Rosalyn Thiro – Blue Island Publishing
Chris Lafbury – Chingford Photographic Society
Kevin Jarman
Douglas Walsh
Mariko Watanabe
Wentworth Golf Hospitality
Crystal Palace National Sports Centre
Sensei Stan Schmidt (JKA South Africa)
Sensei Jim Wood MBE (JKA Scotland)
Aileen Simpson (JKA Scotland)
Sensei Willy Ortiz (JKA Finland)
Sensei Teruyuki Okazaki (ISKF)
Sensei Hiroyoshi Okazaki (ISKF)
Sensei Harry Tagomori PhD (Pacific Shotokan Karate-Do)
Panoramic Visions. USA – www.panoramicvisions.com
Paul Herbert – Dartford Karate Club
Ray Fuller – Thames Karate
Darren Jumnoodoo
Paul Giannandrea
Dr Bill Carr – Transports of Delight
Tim Griffiths (SKD)
Mike Gardener
Bill Cristall
Eric Pich & Sue Sinclair – Kilburn Karate Club
John Cheetham – Shotokan Karate Magazine
Rosemary and Arthur Hall
Tim Ahmet
Cyril Cummings
Simon Bligh
Jim Kelly
Harry Wilson
Rachel Green
Lucy Traettino and Lisa
Gary James
Hachem Salem-Tedj
Stewart Grant
Simon Lailey – Secrets of the Martial Arts
Majo Xeridat

Grateful thanks to the above contributors, all of whom
assisted greatly in the production of this book.

Kind thanks to the editors and publishers of the following publications:

Best Karate Volume 4
By
M. Nakayama
Published by Kodansha
ISBN 4770006861

Meeting Myself – Beyond Spirit of the Empty Hand
By
Stan Schmidt
Published by Focus Publications
ISBN 0911921257

Martial Arts of the Orient
By
Peter Lewis
Published by Ward Lock Ltd
ISBN 0706366418

The Pictorial Guide to the Martial Arts
By
Jim Wilson
Published by Marshall Cavendish Ltd
ISBN 0856851450

ISKF Spotlight

The Evening Standard

Thanks also to the editors and publishers of the following Martial Arts Magazines:

Shotokan Karate Magazine
Traditional Karate
Fighting Arts International
Combat
Karate & Oriental Arts
Dojo Magazine
Martial Arts Today
Arts Martiaux
Arts & Combats

Every effort has been made to trace the picture copyright holders. Karate-London apologises for any unintentional omissions and would be pleased, in such cases, to add an acknowledgment in future editions.

Kind thanks are also offered to all who made contributions to the
Internet Book of Condolence
at
www.karate-london.co.uk

CONTENTS

FOREWORD

In the world of martial arts there is one name that crosses the boundaries of styles, countries and organisations. That of Enoeda. He was respected not by just the followers and supporters of Shotokan Karate, but by all the other leaders of the various martial arts throughout the world. Even the great Sumo team from Japan, upon visiting London, sought out the dojo of Master Enoeda for a visit. He was indeed a true celebrity of the martial arts and a giant figurehead of Shotokan Karate.

The foundations for this book were started between 1990 and 1993, with tape recordings of interviews, photos and notes that were made as a result of my time as a student of Sensei Enoeda. There are nine chapters, which may in some way represent the nine dan grade levels that were awarded to Sensei Enoeda by the JKA.

I feel great sadness that he cannot now see the finished publication, but I hope it stands as a worthy tribute and maybe even a small memorial to our wonderful teacher and our inspiration in the world of karate.

Many close relatives, friends and students of Sensei Enoeda have helped to make the creation of this book possible. There are many, which I have listed, who have helped in lots of different ways with the various tasks and contributions that all go towards the completion of a book. Especial thanks go to Steve Bere, whose design and layout have brought the text and pictures alive. I would also particularly like to thank Mrs Reiko Enoeda, Sensei Yoshinobu Ohta, Sensei Hideo Tomita and Sensei Stan Schmidt for their great assistance and unwavering encouragement in the completion of this book, which I hope you will all enjoy reading and looking at.

Rod Butler – 2003

Introduction by Mrs Reiko Enoeda

It is hard to realise how long it has been since my dear husband Kei passed away.
When I think that I can never again see his shy smiles or hear the sounds of his big laughs,
tears come out and do not stop. I still cannot believe that he is truly gone. He was so full of
energy all the time. I do not want to believe that he is gone.

When I think of him, I try to think of a poem called *A Thousand Winds*.
*"Weep not for me as you stand in front of my tombstone, for I am not in the tomb. I am not
dead. I have become a thousand winds forever blowing around you."* I try to think that my
husband has become a thousand winds, forever blowing around us, protecting us and
giving us his life and energy.

In 1969, we married and went round the small dojos in England to spread the Japanese martial
art called karate, which was almost unknown back then. He loved Japanese food to such an
extent that he could not get sufficient energy without it. So, I had to pack Japanese food along
with an electric rice cooker into our car wherever we went. We made many enjoyable memories
together as well as having some trying times, but all of them seem so distant now. Two years
later, our son Daisuke was born and then our daughter Maya. While I was busy raising them,
my husband travelled extensively to teach karate in the UK and in Europe. He was away from
home about six months of the year. He taught on Saturdays and Sundays as well.
I used to go alone to our children's schools for sports, drama days and PTA meetings. Some
teachers and parents of other pupils thought that I was a single mother! Kei was a very strict
karate teacher but a very loving father for our children. He took us all on holidays
when school was out.

Thirty-five years have passed since then. He was a master of karate and has left us the great
name of Keinosuke Enoeda. Anyone who knows anything about karate will remember this
name, and I am very proud of having been his wife and partner.

Karate is growing ever more popular, and Kei would have been so happy to see it flourish even
further. It was his great dream to see karate as an Olympic sport. However, alas, he is gone. Ten
minutes before he went, he put his thumb up towards me and said, "Daijobu, Daijobu,"
"I will live". He will always live on in our minds and now in the pages of this wonderful book.

It is my great pleasure that this book about my dear husband has been published and I hope that
karate will become even more popular through this book. I would sincerely like to thank
Mr Rod Butler, who has kindly written and published
Keinosuke Enoeda – Tiger of Shotokan Karate.

INOSHISHI
1935: Year of the Wild Boar

EVERY TWELVE YEARS IN JAPAN the year of Inoshishi occurs – the Year of the Wild Boar. The year of Sensei Enoeda's birth, 1935, was Inoshishi, reputably bestowing good luck, success and power upon its male offspring. Sensei Enoeda's incredible success throughout the world could be attributed to the influence of the Wild Boar upon his life; he certainly did have other significant and successful Inoshishi relatives, friends and colleagues who were close to him. Read on, and in the pages ahead, decide for yourself if Inoshishi was indeed the factor that could be credited for the tremendous worldwide success of Sensei Keinosuke Enoeda.

A young Enoeda (far right) training at the JKA Honbu. Note the bandages on the feet

The Enoeda family home in Nogata

It is often thought and written that Keinosuke Enoeda was born in Fukuoka, Japan. This is true to a point. He was born and brought up in Nogata, a town within the prefecture of Fukuoka whose inhabitants were and still are mainly the farming and agricultural community who worked on the land. Nogata is only about a one-and-a-half hour drive from Fukuoka city, so perhaps that is where the confusion arises. The family home was located close to a big river with a large mountainous region nearby, in a farming and agricultural area of Kyushu, the smallest of the three main islands of Japan. This is probably one of the most beneficial positions for a home to be situated; good fortune is said to descend on a home situated in such a location close to water and mountains. Keinsosuke's father, Fukuo Enoeda and his mother, Shikanosuke Yamanaka (her maiden name), were both descendants of ancient Samurai warrior families dating back in Japanese history to the Meiji period.

Enoeda's father, although quite small in build was a

Right **The young Keinosuke with sister Michie**

Below **Keinosuke in his first school photograph**

The young Keinosuke poses for a University photograph

The teenage Enoeda

the first son, Keinosuke, tragically died at just three years of age. The distraught parents desperately wanted another son and when he was eventually born on the 4th July 1935, the name Keinosuke was carried forward and given to him. This is the Keinosuke that we all knew and loved through the years of karate that he gave to us. There was also a sister Michie, four years junior to Keinosuke and a brother Hutoshi who died of a heart attack in 1970 aged just 24 years. Michie Enoeda still lives happily in the family home in Nogata where Keinosuke Enoeda was brought up and spent his early teenage years.

The year of Keinosuke's birth, 1935, was the Year of the Wild Boar, or Inoshishi as it is called in Japan. Inoshishi occurs every 12 years and has special significance for a boy born at this time. The Year of the Wild Boar confers a special luck and power to a male

very keen athlete, a good runner and also a skilled kendoka. (The Kendo that Fukuo Enoeda was skilled at is a vigorous martial art that uses bamboo and steel swords). He also ran a successful trading company specialising in ornamental artefacts, clothing and jewellery. Enoeda's mother died in 1969 at 63 years of age. She spent much of her lifetime caring and looking after her family. There were four children,

born in this year, and Keinosuke Enoeda seemed in every way a typical Inoshishi child awaiting the fabled gifts that Inoshishi conferred. Who could know that this auspicious date of birth would help to carry the young Keinosuke forward to such great success so early in life? And who was so happy that his son had been born in the year of Inoshishi? Fukuo Enoeda was also born in an Inoshishi year and the fact that his

Keinosuke posing for a school photograph

A young Enoeda in a karate class – back row, centre left

**Keinosuke Enoeda's
university days**

**In university uniform with
lifelong friend Matsuo Kon**

his death in 2001 at the age of 90.

Strange as it may seem, the name Enoeda is extremely rare in Japan. If we research the name it means "branches of a large tree", however the Enoeda family tree seems quite small in Japan. There is certainly no record of the name in the Tokyo telephone book. There was at one time, a single entry for the name that could be found in the Kobe telephone book. This entry was for the brother of Sensei Enoeda's father who lived in Kobe, and Sensei Enoeda bore a striking physical resemblance to this close relative of his who died in 1995 aged 85 years. The build and frame of both men carried the same typical Enoeda features.

son was born in the same mythological year carried especial significance and joy to him. Fukuo Enoeda lived to see his son marry and his grandchildren grow up and begin their own working lives. He also saw the worldwide success of his son Keinosuke before

Keinosuke Enoeda in traditional uniform with the university sumo team

Living in the country it was quite natural for the young Keinosuke to take to sports as a means of fun and entertainment. At primary school he loved baseball and enjoyed playing daily. At high school he went on to study judo and kendo, showing a natural ability for martial arts at this young age and gaining his black belt in judo at the age of 15. He loved judo and began to excel in the martial art eventually reaching Judo 2nd Dan (2nd degree level) at 17 years of age. He was also successful on the judo competition circuit and became runner up in the All Japan High School Judo Championships. There is evidence that the young Enoeda also had some experience of karate before attending Takushoku University, where it is generally recognised that he began his formal training in Shotokan Karate. Look at the picture on the left of a very young Enoeda in a karate class; the stance and the block

Makiwara training was a daily ritual for Keinosuke

appear to show quite a bit of skill at what must have been some time before university studies.

Those first early steps in judo laid the basic foundations for his love of the martial arts, and when he later saw a spectacular display of karate almost by accident at an open day of the Takushoku University in Tokyo, the young Enoeda was hooked. Master Irea and Okazaki put on a display of JKA karate that left the audience spellbound and also made a lasting impression on the young Enoeda. (Seek out any early pictures or films of these two great JKA instructors and it is very easy to see why.) This was unfortunately the point when judo lost a young and powerful champion black belt to karate at just 17 years of age.

The choice of university for Enoeda was a foregone conclusion. Takushoku had a reputation for strong and successful martial arts and it was here that he enrolled for his further educational studies.

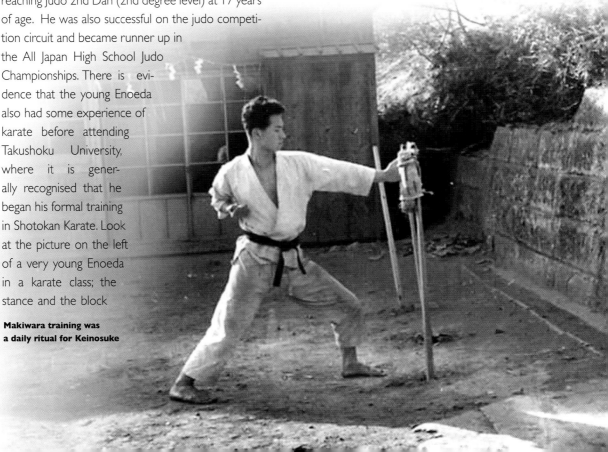

It was rare for a student to be selected for any of the university martial arts teams during their first year. Usually one had to wait until at least the second year had started and evidence given that skills in the martial arts were firmly established. Enoeda was selected in his first year at Takushoku, such was the undeniable belief in his ability by his seniors. His skills on the competition circuit were honed during these years at university. The East of Japan Tournament, the West of Japan Tournament and the All Japan Universities Championship were all regular venues for the Takushoku karate team. There were also inter university tournaments during the academic year and

an age-old rivalry between Takushoku University (Shotokan) and Nichidai University (Wado-Ryu). Enoeda took them all in his stride and enhanced his skills and fast growing reputation along the way.

On 27th November 1955, after studying karate for two years at Takushoku, he passed his first-degree Shodan Black Belt examination. The entry in the JKA register gives a record of the number 1,200 that was registered against his name. There had been 1,199 successful Shodans previously registered. During this time he rapidly made a reputation in the karate club for being a strong and determined fighter, and Master Funakoshi Gichin would often be taking these classes, which the young Enoeda greatly enjoyed.

**Takushoku University Judo
Team Captain (left) and
Karate Team Captain (right)**

Keinosuke Enoeda's university days with good friend Matsuo Kon (top row centre), and Shiro Asano (bottom row centre). Both of these friends from Takushoku University went on to become very successful karate instructors in their own right

Reiko's father Rikimatsu Hayashi, with Keinosuke's father Fukuo

January 1969: Hutoshi Enoeda, who died just one year later aged 24, Reiko Hayashi (who shortly became Mrs Enoeda), Keinsosuke's father Fukuo and Reiko's father Rikimatsu Hayashi

Three generations of Enoeda: Keinosuke with his father Fukuo, his son Daisuke and his sister Michie at the Nogata Shrine in Kyushu, Japan

Training would be daily at 6.00a.m. before university studies and again at 8.00p.m. after studies. He also attended the afternoon club, which ran for two hours after university work. There would also be daily practise on the makiwara (striking pad), which over the years developed his incredible striking power and strengthened the reputation of the Enoeda punch. With this intensive regime of more than five hours daily training, progress was, by our standards, extremely fast. On 23rd November 1956 aged just 21 he became No.333 in the list of JKA Nidans or second-degree black belts. Shortly after this his efforts and skills were further rewarded when he was made captain of the Takushoku University karate club.

He graduated in 1957 with a degree in Commerce, but one wonders if the main reason for choosing Takushoku was not the academic standards of the institution but the karate and the powerful martial arts programme within the university, together with the desire to emulate the skills of Irea and Okazaki that had captured Enoeda's imagination and held him hostage. Enoeda had got his degree, but had his mind on other things. He had caught the attention of the great Masatoshi Nakayama and was invited to attend the famed and elite three-year JKA Instructors Class at the JKA Honbu in Tokyo. Those next three years would see the sharpening of the blade and the strengthening of the steel.

The
ENOEDA
ERA

T HE WORLD WAS IN FOR A SHOCK.
Enoeda stamped his trademark Samurai
spirit on all corners of the globe. During
the forty years of the Enoeda Era it is doubtful
if there was any country to which the name and
reputation of Enoeda did not reach.

**Karate action at
Seymour Hall in London**

Completing the Three Year JKA Instructors Course (which was originated by the late Master Masatoshi Nakayama) was like an apprenticeship for Enoeda, giving him the foundation of teaching skills that he later developed into his own personal style. As well as the extreme physical demands of the course there was also theory and knowledge to assimilate. Deep knowledge of the mechanics of the body, and a thorough understanding of the katas and their applications were essential. Masters Nakayama and Nishiyama regularly tested the graduates of this programme on their understanding of this knowledge and the terminology involved. The Instructors Course produced many Japanese and indeed some non-Japanese instructors who would later become

karate ambassadors, introducing JKA Shotokan Karate to the rest of the world. Masters Ochi, Okazaki, Mikami, Shirai, Kase, Yahara, Kanazawa, Mori and many others together with Enoeda all travelled the world and made bases for themselves in various countries teaching karate.

After successfully completing the JKA Instructors Course, Enoeda was still hungry for further success and fulfilment. He aimed to win the All Japan Championships and began preparations to realise this, his next great ambition. The preparations for the Championships, which Enoeda began in 1960, put the wheels in motion for what was to become one of the greatest periods of time in karate history – the Enoeda Era.

Celebrating his 1963 success with karate colleagues

Yoko Tobi Geri

The Enoeda Era stretched for forty years from the day he won the All Japan Championships in 1963 to the day he died in 2003. His star was burning brightly and he successfully took his Sandan (3rd Degree Black Belt) grading examination on 13th June 1960, with the JKA registered pass number of 150. Almost exactly two years later on 12th June 1962 he achieved the level of Yondan (4th Degree Black Belt) and became Yondan number 63 in the JKA records. The intensity of training must have been extreme to achieve this level of skill in such a relatively short period of time, however the catalyst that shot Enoeda onto the world stage and changed the course of the history of karate was not the dan gradings but the 1963 All Japan Championships. Held at the Metropolitan Gymnasium in Tokyo, this highly prestigious event for karate was, and to this day still is, the touchstone for rivalries between the many clubs and universities in Japan all vying for positions in the finals.

Competition was fierce amongst these various karate groups and even fiercer between the individuals in these groups. However, Enoeda had made a decision – the decision to win at all costs. The earlier 1961 championships saw him slowly work his way to the finals, taking third place in the individual Kumite event together with Mikami. Shirai took second place, and Asai won the event. In 1962 the story was similar, but Enoeda had been there before. He knew what to prepare for and had one more year's experience and time for preparations. He took second place against Shirai, who won, pushing Mikami and Yaguchi into third place. The 1963 All Japan Championships, held at the Tokyo Metropolitan Gymnasium, saw Enoeda who was then a tough 4th Dan, in his prime. After the two previous years in the finals, he took first place, beating Shirai who came second, and Kanazawa and Yaguchi who came third. Enoeda's first score against Shirai in the finals was Mae Geri for which he was awarded an ippon. He then finished the match with a second ippon given for a devastating Gyaku Zuki. As well as being a win for Enoeda, this was also a win for Takushoku University, an old rival to Komazawa University, which was where Shirai studied and trained. Master Nakayama described this final as "one of the finest there has ever been". At 27 years of age Enoeda's confidence was now unshakeable and his determination unbreakable. At this time Jitte was his favourite kata, which took him to a very respectable fourth place in the All Japan finals. However, he wanted the Kumite title and he got it!

After losing the 1963 title to Enoeda, Shirai worked and studied ways to defend against the Mae Geri of Enoeda. He practised Gedan Barai over and over again on a daily basis working to increase the speed and efficiency of his defence at different angles and distances. When the two met in later championships, Enoeda didn't use the Mae Geri again, but craftily scored with lightening fast hand techniques. It is interesting to note that a special bond was formed between these two competitors, and that many years later Shirai would be invited as a special guest instructor to many of the annual JKA European courses, organised by Enoeda and held at Crystal Palace in London.

With Sensei Stan Schmidt, who became the JKA chief instructor in South Africa

The 1963 event set the seal on Enoeda's future as a top ranked, world-class competitor and instructor, and it was this reputation that preceded him on his travels to various countries around the world and eventually to England. Years later I asked him how he approached the 1963 championships and if he made any mental preparations for the event apart from the physical preparations he had made. His face changed. He looked me in the eyes with defiance and a seriousness that was quite unnerving. "I told myself I had to win. If I lost I would have to give up karate, I would never be able to go back and show my face at the dojo!"

With this Samurai warrior spirit he took the title, and karate gained one of the most legendary and charismatic figures that there has ever been. In some ways, this uncompromising attitude laid the foundation for the following years, which were to become known as the Enoeda Era.

Sensei Nakayama commented that Enoeda always fought like a tiger; the term was seized upon by the karate establishment, and Enoeda soon became known as Tora – "Tiger" in Japan, a nickname gained  for his ferocious and skilled fighting abilities. Enoeda also carried another token of praise. He was twenty-seven, a young, fast and strong 4th Dan fresh from the JKA Instructors Course and by this time he had also earned himself the reputation of having the "strongest punch in the world". This reputation was started by many of his opponents whom he come up against on his way to the finals in 1961, 1962 and 1963 and was endorsed by many of his subsequent opponents. Enoeda's daily practice at the makiwara had paid off and he continued his daily ritual on the makiwara right up until the end of his life.

Sensei Stan Schmidt of South Africa recalls the time when he first met Master Enoeda. "My first visit

Yoko Tobi Geri

teaching ability as for his reputation as a fighter. This was an incredible period of growth in fame for Enoeda, who then became in demand throughout the world as a teacher of karate.

The next forty years were also a great period of growth for karate throughout the world, as karate in the 1950s and 1960s had been viewed purely as an offshoot of judo or jujitsu. Following this time when karate had a very small following, it grew to a point where almost every town and city in the UK and indeed throughout the world had two or three thriving karate clubs. Much of this was due to Enoeda, his dynamic karate and his charismatic personality. It is doubtful if there will ever be a period of growth such as this again throughout the world for Japanese martial arts.

to Japan was for three months starting April 1963 at the Honbu Dojo in Yottsuya. I trained with the general class and later was invited to train with the instructors class. Enoeda Sensei had seen me doing kumite with a senior black belt whom I managed to do well against, and both he and Shirai Sensei recommended that I be promoted from 7th kyu to 3rd kyu after taking an intensive grading test. It was then that Enoeda Sensei took me under his wing, saying to me, "I like your fighting spirit, so I will coach you every day after class". It was very hard training, where he slapped my limbs around in his friendly and boisterous way literally moulding me into shape. This resulted in my inviting him to teach at my dojo in South Africa, which he later did." Stan also took part in the 1963 Sixth All Japan Championships in Tokyo, providing the chair demonstration with colleague Tom Ryan. The chair display started off with the chairs being used as seats and finished with the chairs being used as weapons to attack each other with! ABC-TV filmed the highlights of the championships, including Enoeda's winning match in the finals, together with Stan's chair display.

By now Enoeda's reputation as the tiger with the strongest punch in the world was seized upon by the karate press as word spread about the incredible capabilities of this karate champion. However, this reputation did not do justice to the other side of his abilities. Enoeda's skills as a teacher actually overtook these flamboyant and headline-grabbing descriptions, and he was sought out as much for his

After he won the All Japan Championships in 1963, everyone sat up and took notice of this young and dynamic athlete of karate with a reputation that ran before him like the tidal wave in Hokusai's famous painting. One very special man who was in the audience of the 1963 All Japan Championships and who did sit up and take notice was President Achmad Sukarno, the president of Indonesia. He took a great interest in Enoeda and the results of the finals, and he was to have a great influence and a far reaching effect on the future of the new champion and his career as a karate instructor. President Sukarno was so impressed with Enoeda's skills that he began negotiations straightaway with Master Nakayama to bring Enoeda over to Indonesia.

The negotiations were successful and for the last

An early picture of masters Kase, Enoeda and Shirai during the world tour 1965

four months of 1963, Master Nakayama together with Enoeda were working guests of the President in Indonesia. They were teaching the skills of unarmed combat not only to the President's bodyguards but also to the police. The lessons were going particularly well, and as a celebration President Sukarno arranged a special feast to which Sensei Enoeda was to be the guest of honour.

One of the courses of that meal took the form of a bowl of white jelly-like substance. Sensei Enoeda ate this rather strange tasting dish and then enquired as to what it was. The President's wife Debbie, previously a presenter on Japanese TV and something of a celebrity, explained that the dish was monkey brain, a real delicacy, very expensive and reserved only for special guests!

The embryonic seeds of karate had been sown during World War 2 and afterwards in the 1940s and 1950s. America, particularly, was fertile ground for these ideas to propagate, and servicemen returned to their homelands from their duties in Japan and Okinawa enthusing about the martial arts that they had seen and experienced. It was only a matter of time before karate and indeed other martial arts sprang to life and demanded knowledge and attention. Enoeda's timing was perfect; he was just what America, Europe, Africa and Asia were looking for. These continents now had a hunger and a thirst for the knowledge, skills and experience that Enoeda

possessed, and he set about serving these demands by touring these continents and administering his medicine.

Master Nakayama was the key to this pheonmenal growth of karate and with great foresight he organised a tour taking Enoeda, Kanazawa, Shirai, Mori and Kase to the four corners of the world. As Master Gichin Funakoshi had done in 1922 when he introduced karate to mainland Japan from Okinawa, so Master Nakayama did again, but this time on a larger, pan-global scale.

On 8th March 1964, Enoeda successfully passed his 5th Dan grading examination, becoming number 25, only the 25th instructor in the world to have gained this grade. The world beckoned, and after stretches of teaching karate at the JKA in Tokyo and at Tokyo Art School during 1964, the world karate tour commenced in March 1965. The countries to be visited were South Africa, Hawaii, Los Angeles,

A warm welcome for Sensei Enoeda in South Africa

New York, Philadelphia and on to Europe, taking in Germany, Belgium, France, Holland and England.

The first six months were spent in South Africa, with Sensei Kanazawa going on to teach in Pretoria, Kase to Durban and Shirai to Cape Town. Enoeda stayed for six months in Johannesburg at the home of Sensei Stan Schmidt, the JKA Chief Instructor in South Africa. Stan acted as host to Sensei Enoeda and recalls vividly his first impressions. "Enoeda Sensei arrived in the country looking like a Samurai, unmarried and head shaven – tough looking, like a gladiator." "Enoeda Sensei's first lesson at our dojo in 1965 was unforgettable. He ordered "Kiba Dachi Kamai!" We all did Kiba Dachi then he shouted "more down!". This was not enough so he kicked each of us in the stomach and shouted "more down!" even louder, and then we understood. The first impression of all the students was one of awe, fascination and hero worship as they had never seen such dynamic punches, kicks and strikes."

The Japanese team of instructors also performed spectacular demonstrations at various venues in South Africa, and Enoeda taught afternoons and evenings on a daily basis in Johannesburg. Stan Schmidt recalls his own daily personal training with Sensei Enoeda. "We would rise at 6.00am every morning and train outside in the garden or drive to the park. Our outdoor training included hand hardening on different kinds of makiwara, either an upright pole planted in the ground with a pad on it, or various trees, large or small. We did front kicks, side kicks and back kicks delivered with running shoes on against the trunk of an old oak tree. Roundhouse kicks we did against leaves. We did fast repetitive snapping kicks while keeping the knee elevated and always finished our training with Kata." Stan recalls these times with great affection and told a story about one of his very first experiences with Enoeda Sensei. "I remember well when he first arrived in South Africa. It was the first Thursday after his arrival and he called me to his room, poured me a beer and informed me that Fridays would be the days we did one hour kumite at the dojo. Then he raised his beer glass and shouted "Kampai" (cheers). With all my previous bravado I hardly slept that night, knowing that I would have to confront the All Japan Champion (1963) on my own every Friday. I

**Sensei Enoeda and
Sensei Stan Schmidt**

remembered very clearly his comments about his time on the Instructors Course at the JKA honbu''; "Maybe some instructors happy I leave Japan. My spirit maybe sometime too strong. Maybe too much like old Samurai spirit. Some instructors not like this. I like hard kumite – must be real – sometimes injury happen. I try study Ashi-Barai, many times I practise on my student's ankle. He tie big padding around ankle, and so I like sweeping! When fighting, I not like sweeping one leg; I like to sweep both legs! One time my opponent stand, not move, I sweep, he fall down. I very sorry, his leg broken. This is kumite!"

"I shuddered to think what might happen to me if the Tiger attacked me with his formidable leg sweep,, but my thoughts were then interrupted with the pleasant description of a tooth extraction job he had performed on one of his other opponents."

"He move in to attack me – Ah, perfect timing, I see perfect distance. I release Gyaku-Zuki – perfect power. Perfect control from me, but he make little mistake. He jerk his head maybe two centimetres forward as I punch. I think maybe just a little touch and everything OK. Then I hear sound like not cooked rice falling on wooden floor. Very strange. I quickly look in his mouth. All his top teeth still in mouth, but they not so long anymore. Very clean break. Bottom half of teeth now lying on floor. Why this happen? Me not understand. This very funny."

Stan continued his story; "I survived the weekly kumite sessions, but after 2 months of gruelling training just prior to the first SA Championships Enoeda Sensei landed a kakato (heel kick) in the centre of my thigh which was very painful. I was limping as I carried on fighting but it was not easy driving my car afterwards. Enoeda Sensei volunteered quite confidently – "I drive! But you please teach me". "At first my Volvo bucked along like a wild bronco, with me less worried about my leg and more worried about the clutch of my automobile. By the time we reached my house Sensei seemed to have mastered the gentle art of driving very well indeed."

"Enoeda Sensei loved eating and drinking a large variety of food and beverages and was always laughing, encouraging and challenging karateka to higher levels shouting "More spirit!" I never saw him overindulge in food or drink at any stage. He was quick to tell us what he liked and at breakfast he used to make a concoction of steamed rice mixed with 2 raw eggs, grated cheese and whatever cold meat was available such as diced chicken, beef or salami. Over this he would pour Kikkoman soya sauce, which a Japanese family residing in South Africa had given him. My wife, my daughters and myself were all eventually consuming what we called the Enoeda Special."

"On one occasion we telephoned Japan, and the secretary at the Honbu Dojo, Maya-san said, "Please tell Enoeda to come back because everything is so quiet at Honbu Dojo now that he is gone." By the

way, Enoeda Sensei when talking to his friends on the phone didn't really need a telephone – he would talk so loudly that one could hear his voice outside at the swimming pool! We also played quite a lot of golf and quite often he would make a kiai when making a drive and give us all a fright. Everybody loved him. Once at a resort, a group of karateka took him swimming. They were sitting in a group deeply engrossed in what he was telling them when suddenly he turned to Cecil Wolov and said, pointing to the pool, "Child drowning, you save!". One of the guys dived in and saved the child.

This was Enoeda – full of life, highly communicative, aware and sharp as a razor. Sensei Enoeda helped greatly to establish the JKA in South Africa, he was a special friend and in many ways I regarded him as my brother."

"Enoeda's second visit occurred in 1972, seven years after his first visit. He brought with him his wife, Reiko, and his baby son, Daisuke. Gone was the spiky, short-cropped head and that cavalier bachelor swagger. What entered our home was a well groomed English gentleman and family man. This was off the dojo floor, of course. On the floor he was still as potent as ever. During his stay, an incident occurred that I will never forget."

"It was a warm lazy Friday afternoon, about 4 o'clock. We'd had a tough week of teaching and touring the country, and we were enjoying a well-earned rest, when I received a call from my receptionist at the Orange Grove Dojo. "Stan, there are two men here to see you." I replied,. "Tell them to come on Monday, I'm

Sensei Enoeda in South Africa with Sensei Stan Schmidt

Many of the world's top instructors at the Masters Camp in the USA. Front row: Sensei Gneo, Enoeda, Okazaki, Ueki & Schmidt. Back row: Sensei Takashina, Mikami, Koyama & Yaguchi

resting." My receptionist sounded concerned. "Stan,, the one who is very aggressive says he's come to challenge you to a fight." I turned to Enoeda Sensei, who had just showered and was reading a book and I quickly told him what was happening. "Stan, go kick him!" he shouted without any hesitation. "You want me to come?" "No, Sensei, there's only one guy." "Okay. You go. Come back soon." Back at home after I had sorted the problem out, Enoeda asked me what had happened. "I kicked his butt." "Good, Stan," he laughed and poured me a beer. "This also happened to me before." "What happened, Sensei?" "When I was first in London, some crazy guy came to my new dojo at Marshall Street, Piccadilly. He wanted to fight me. He said he studied karate in China and Korea. I told him "OK, but you must first take training. After class I will fight you." "Very good idea Sensei." I laughed. Enoeda was grinning from ear to ear. "Yes, Stan, because I gave a very sweat-up class. Many geri, zuki and squat and kick training. Then we did five-step sparring. I watched him. Very strong, but he telegraphed before stepping, so, I joined the line." This I liked. How cunning and wise the Sensei is I thought. "Then what, Sensei?" "He was at the end of the line, I was on the other side. Maybe 20 black belts in class. I say "change" many times and soon he was standing and facing me. Now I shout, "Ippon

Kumite!" (one-step sparring). I count, Itchi! (One!). He attack jodan (face level). I block and say, "Again, you no good balance. You try again!" Now all class is watching. I see his face puff up like a blowfish. I count, "Ni!" (Two!). He made a swinging attack to my face. I jumped back. He missed, but he became very angry when I asked him, "Why you so slow?" He lost his temper and attacked me before I could make a count. But I made a good timing Mae-Geri to his stomach. My kick was not so hard, but he fell down to the floor. I helped him up. His face was very grey. He looked sick and I helped him to lie down on a bench. Then I told him, "OK, I am ready to fight you now! Very funny, Stan. This big man, he cried out like baby, "No! No! Please, no!" "And?" I prompted. "He never came back to my dojo again." "I wonder why, Sensei."

By this time Enoeda had decided to make a successful and solid base for himself in the United Kingdom. His initial visit in 1965 led him shortly afterwards to settle permanently in the country that he grew to love. During 1966 and 1967 before settling down permanently in England, he travelled extensively throughout America teaching on courses and in training camps with Master Nishiyama and other JKA instructors.

Sensei Willy J. Ortiz of JKA Finland recalls this time in America. "I met him in 1965 while living in New

York City; together with Sensei Okazaki and Kizaka, he helped to built the New York Karate Club until the arrival of Sensei Mori in 1967. We liked each other from the beginning, because we both were very serious about our intentions towards karate. Our ways were separated until 1975 when I came to live in Finland and joined EAKF, later ESKA. Throughout the years our friendship became closer, to the point where we shared some very interesting conversations, laughing at jokes and talking about our families and, of course, karate. While visiting Finland he stayed at my home and I introduced him to "Finnish sauna"."

I was interested in this link with New York and Finland and enquired as to how the relationship started. Sensei Ortiz explained. "The first time I met Sensei Enoeda, he was standing by the door of the New York Karate Club waiting for somebody to open the door, for which I had the key. He seemed quite restless, like a tiger in a cage waiting to get free. Now that I think about it, I can understand why they called him "Tora". I didn't know much about him, but I had heard about him coming from Philadelphia to give us a lesson; guessing

Sensei Enoeda with Willy Ortiz in Finland

correctly, I introduced myself and since it was still one hour before training I invited him to have a cup of coffee. His serious face changed to a friendly smiling face and we spent our first half hour talking about Japan and Perú, my birthplace. No karate."

"In those days I was a green belt from Sensei Hiroshi Orito. Frankly I don't remember what that first lesson

Sensei Mori, Ortiz and Enoeda in Finland 1991

was about, but I remember the warm-up was beyond what I had experienced up until then. There was this young instructor (29 years old) who hardly could speak English and he was pushing us beyond any one of our limits. I was very impressed by his performance, and that experience made my resolution to become an instructor even stronger. He came many times to New York Karate Club alone and also together with Senseis Katsuya Kizaka and Teruyuki Okazaki. By then I knew what to expect from him and thus technically I developed and our conversations became more friendly, but it didn't affect his rough handling of me during the class when I made mistakes!"

"In 1966 the All American Karate Championships were held in New York and there I saw him spar with the American star of kumite, Frank Smith. It happened during a belt test, with Sensei Nishiyama being the Chief Instructor. Enoeda Sensei was called to take Frank's kumite test. Faster than my eyes could see, I saw a white blur going up and down and next thing I saw was Frank on his knees holding his jaw and a repentant looking Enoeda standing by him. I think he was very embarrassed. Some forty

Sensei Mori, Ortiz and Enoeda

Allan Smith, one of Enoeda's first students in England

years later he told me so himself." "I was very embarrassed by my lack of control."

"In 1967 Sensei Masataka Mori came from Hawaii to take charge of our club and soon afterwards the rumours of Sensei Enoeda leaving the USA for England started to spread. His final lesson was nice: we performed Sochin kata for over an hour and after the regular free style we went down to our favorite bar, Tip Top". After a few beers we shook hands and he left."

"In 1975 I moved to live in Finland and since then I have had many opportunities to sit down with Sensei and talk about all kind of things from karate to golf and from his family to mine. He liked to sing, but above all he liked to listen when my brother Mike and I sang some Peruvian songs. In his final visit to Finland we sat down in front of all the practitioners and while I sang a few songs with my brother he sat by me and smiled with a glass of beer in his hand; after a while I asked him to sing *Suki Yaki* and he did so in a beautiful form. THEN I gave some explanation in Finnish language to my students and at the end of this explanation they all laughed and Sensei got very curious. After a few seconds he asked, "What did you tell them?". I was a bit afraid of his reaction but I considered him my friend more than a Sensei and I had to tell him the truth. "I told them that you were called the Tiger of Shotokan and that you were a great man, but I was

greater because I had made a tiger sing." He choked himself laughing and I thought that this is what a Sensei should look and feel like. He had developed so much from the first time I met him."

Sensei Enoeda returned to England in 1968 after his time in America and replaced Sensei Kanazawa who was the JKA Chief Instructor at this time. A temporary home was made in Liverpool where there was a strong interest in karate. His accommodation comprised of a flat based at Percy Street in the centre of Liverpool. He inspired some of the early pioneers of karate in the north of England such as Andy Sherry, Bob Poynton, Terry O'Neill, Bill Crystal, and many others, with his unique and powerful style of karate and his dynamic teaching skills. Someone who became an immediate devotee of Enoeda was Allan Smith from Liverpool. Allan could well hold the record of being the very first student of Sensei Enoeda in England.

Enoeda lived for one year in Liverpool and the early mornings would often be spent running and training in the park with some of the keenest students. This was the open-air training that Enoeda

Sensei Enoeda with a very young Andy Sherry

Gyaku Zuki in Liverpool

Sensei Hideto Matsui

enjoyed so much wherever he was based during the whole of his life. As well as teaching regularly on a daily basis at the Liverpool Red Triangle Dojo, there were these special early morning 7.00am sessions at Sefton Park, Liverpool, in the open air, which many of the keenest students always attended. True to style, Enoeda would always grab the opportunity to train in the open whenever possible.

Shotokan Karate was slowly growing in popularity in Great Britain, and the British Karate Federation, which had been in existence since the 1950s, developed into the KUGB, which was formed in 1966. The British Karate Federation was responsible for Kanazawa's time in the country and the early growth and interest of karate throughout England. The early pioneers in Liverpool and London formed the backbone of the KUGB – The Karate Union of Great Britain, that at its peak a few years later with Enoeda as its figurehead, boasted well over 20,000 members and more than 450 clubs.

At around this point in time a young businessman arrived from Japan. A graduate of Yokohama University and a keen JKA karate practitioner, Hideto Matsui sought out the presence of Sensei Enoeda to continue with his karate studies and practise in England. Matsui was sent to Liverpool by his bank in Japan to study at Liverpool University. He became part of the developing karate infrastructure in the Liverpool area and formed friendships with Andy Sherry, Bob Poynton, Bill Crystal, Sandy Hopkins, Steve Cattle, Terry O'Neill and Bob Rhodes. Sensei Matsui taught in many of the karate clubs in the north of England during his time in the country and formed a lifelong friendship with Sensei Enoeda. Enoeda was

The wedding day of Keinosuke and Reiko Enoeda

exactly 12 years older than Matsui. This may not be of significance to a non-Japanese person but it meant that Matsui, who was at that time a 3rd Dan, was also born in the year of INOSHISHI. A very special bond was formed between the two. Enoeda took the young Matsui under his wing and a lifelong friendship began. Sensei Matsui, who I first met whilst he was teaching on the 2003 Sensei Enoeda Memorial Course at Crystal Palace, recalled those early days with great fondness. "Sensei Enoeda was so energetic, always on the move. He felt like an older brother to me and acted as a close advisor and helper in my life." At this point I secretly wondered if Sensei Enoeda also saw in the young Hideto, a likeness to the two brothers he had lost earlier in his own life? Sensei Matsui is now the Director of Nippon Computer Systems Corporation in Japan and a 6th Dan karate instructor.

During the 1960s, further south in London, the early pioneers of karate were the late Eddie Whitcher, Mick Randall, John van Weenen, the late Harry Jones and Greg Durant. They were largely inspired by Sensei Kanazawa, who taught more towards the south of England during his residency. The late Vernon Bell was responsible for bringing over to the UK Sensei Kanazawa and some of the very first Japanese JKA instructors during the 1950s and 1960s. These were the formative years for karate in the United Kingdom,, which initiated a much wider interest in karate during later years. In 1968 after Sensei Kanazawa left England

to become the Chief Instructor in Germany, Sensei Enoeda became the Chief Instructor to the KUGB and subsequently moved south to create a base in London. His early dojos at that time were situated at Blackfriars in a church hall and at the Budokwai in Kensington, West London. The Budokwai is the oldest martial arts dojo in England and has a long history of judo and karate activities. Dave Hazzard, together with Pauline and Ray Fuller were early devotees of Sensei Enoeda at that time and now have their own successful karate organisations. There was also a dojo in Seymour Hall in the West End of London for a while, but problems with the neighbours ensured that this was never going to be a permanent site for an Enoeda dojo.

This picture of the Marshall Street Dojo shows many of the early stalwarts of karate in London. Ray Fuller and Dave Hazzard are in the line-up

Worldwide success for the KUGB team

On the 17th May 1969 Keinosuke Enoeda married Reiko Hayashi and the happy couple set up home in Richmond, Surrey. Reiko recalls the early days when she first met her future husband. "Keinosuke was from the south of Japan and I was from Tokyo, much further north. I had great difficulty in understanding his accent and would often ask him to repeat something he had said. He would lose patience and say, "No! I've said it now – enough!" The new Mrs Enoeda was very homesick after leaving her home and her family in Japan to live in England. She recalls, "I found England cold and had few friends at that time. I wanted to go back to Japan." Reiko travelled everywhere with her new husband before their first baby, Daisuke, was born. She would take along all the materials and utensils to ensure that her husband had his proper Japanese meals. It is true to say that although Sensei Enoeda enjoyed England and the English people, he did not have the same enthusiasm for English food. He could not understand why a pudding was made out of rice, something that should be used for sushi or eaten, boiled or steamed with the main meal. The couple would stay in students' homes or in a guest house or hotel, but always the rice and traditional Japanese food would be prepared and made ready by Reiko.

At one point Reiko suggested to her husband that it might be a sensible idea for her to learn karate, as she did accompany him to many of the clubs and dojos.

Daily practise of the basics

The conversation went like this. Reiko: "I want to learn karate." Sensei Enoeda: "No! It would be very embarrassing, so please don't try."

On the 1st April 1970, 6th Dan was awarded to Sensei Enoeda. The number in the JKA records in Tokyo shows the registration as number 25.

Sensei Enoeda loved England and called it the "Greatest Karate Nation in the World". He regularly took part in sporting activities apart from his karate and golf. At 6.30am most mornings, he would be swimming and then fitness training. There was even a makiwara set up in the garage of the family home that was always used when he was not at the dojo. He loved taking part in sport and also watching it, however the one sport he did not like or show any interest in was cricket. He enjoyed horseracing and every year would take his wife Reiko to Epsom for a special day out at the races, dressed in top hat and all of the essential racegoers' clothing.

Their son, Daisuke, was born on 31st December 1971 at 7.30am. This, the couple's first baby, was due on 7th January 1972, but the father-to-be was not happy about this

**Enoeda always thrilled with his
spectacular karate displays**

particular date. Sensei Enoeda wanted an Inoshishi baby, which had to be born at least a week earlier before the end of December. Reiko duly obliged and with the promise of a fur coat as an incentive, went into labour and gave birth to the baby Daisuke on the last day of December 1971. On enquiring later about the promised fur coat, Sensei Enoeda produced what looked like a genuine fur coat upon his return from a trip to Scotland. Reiko remembers. "It looked like rabbit! Horrible! All the fur kept coming out and sticking to everything. He went to great effort to get it, but I could not wear it." It later transpired that the coat had been bought in a sale.

The Enoeda family was completed by the birth of a daughter, Maya, almost exactly four years later on 14th December 1975. For 12 years there was also a cherished family dog, a male Collie that was named "Laddie". The dog was subsequently renamed "Lassie" by school friends of Maya, in spite of the fact that "Lassie" was a male dog!

Sensei Enoeda took to the English way of life and enjoyed it greatly. He received offers from other countries to take up residence with them, but always declined and stayed at his base in England.

He made many friends in the UK, particularly with the leaders of the other styles of martial arts. There was much socialising, together with games of Mah Jong and always a good rapport between these karate teachers. There was a healthy competitiveness particularly between Sensei Enoeda and Sensei Suzuki, the chief instructor of the Wado Ryu style of karate in the UK. In the 1970s competitions were staged between the various styles, notably a large

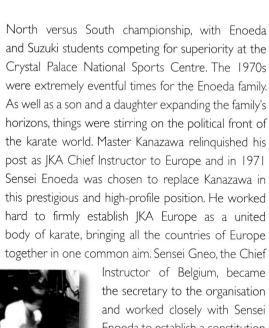

North versus South championship, with Enoeda and Suzuki students competing for superiority at the Crystal Palace National Sports Centre. The 1970s were extremely eventful times for the Enoeda family. As well as a son and a daughter expanding the family's horizons, things were stirring on the political front of the karate world. Master Kanazawa relinquished his post as JKA Chief Instructor to Europe and in 1971 Sensei Enoeda was chosen to replace Kanazawa in this prestigious and high-profile position. He worked hard to firmly establish JKA Europe as a united body of karate, bringing all the countries of Europe together in one common aim. Sensei Gneo, the Chief Instructor of Belgium, became the secretary to the organisation and worked closely with Sensei Enoeda to establish a constitution and rules for JKA Europe.

In 1973 a permanent London Dojo was found for Sensei Enoeda at Marshall Street Baths

Karate action at Seymour Hall, London

and Leisure Centre in London's West End. This venue became an attraction for karate students from around the world, as well as a permanent base for Enoeda from which to operate. In 1974 Sensei Enoeda returned to Japan for a short visit. On the 1st December whilst in Japan he was awarded 7th Dan, the JKA number? – 21.

Meanwhile, back in England, the KUGB with the assistance of Sensei Enoeda started going from strength to strength, and the membership grew to enormous proportions. International success followed success at home and the young KUGB star Frank Brennan together with others such as Terry O'Neill, Andy Sherry and many members of the KUGB teams, became known world-wide for their skills and successes on the championship circuit. Sensei Enoeda would travel regularly to the Red Triangle Dojo in Liverpool to conduct the KUGB squad training. He inspired countless numbers of squad members to achieve extremely high standards resulting in success, both at home and abroad. This success reached a peak when in 1990 England beat Japan in the finals at the world karate championships held in Sunderland, England. It is probably fair to say that most of the senior karate instructors in England today who have their own organisations were once part of the vast KUGB or British Karate Federation network of clubs. Enoeda's face and image were used extensively on the KUGB publicity. Posters, leaflets and books were all produced incorporating the famous Mawashi Geri and Kizami Zuki of Enoeda, expertly photographed by Bernard Rose. The KUGB became an extremely dominant force on the world karate stage.

The KUGB National Championships held for many years at Crystal Palace and previously at Alexandra Palace in London was the showcase for some of the best karate in England. The event was always sold out in advance and many other associations' members and chief instructors would always be seen in the

Terry O'Neill, Ray Kerridge, Hugh Achilles and Sensei Tomita all attack Sensei Enoeda in an early karate display at Seymour Hall in London

audience. The event was brilliantly organised and as well as seeing some of the world's top competitors, Sensei Enoeda's special karate display would always be eagerly awaited. There would be a fanfare of horns by uniformed musicians, plus dramatic lighting and sound effects to add to the excitement of the evening. Master Enoeda would then enter the arena, dressed in his traditional black Hakama. The introduction to this part of the evening was made by Mrs Buck, Sensei's secretary, who would also explain the meaning behind the musical accompaniment. His own unique kata would be performed to the sound of some very special Japanese music. The music for the display, *Karate-Do HITOTSUJI*, was written by the famous Japanese musician, I. George. I. George was

in fact a student of Sensei Enoeda in Japan who became a popular musician and singer. The lyrics for the music were written by Sensei Takagi, who was previously the managing director of the JKA. The meaning of the lyrics emphasise complete dedication to the spirituality of Karate-Do. The whole piece of music was written as a dedication to Sensei Enoeda, a man who has put his whole heart and soul into his training. The title *Karate-Do HITOTSUJI* literally means "the way of the essence of karate". The special kata, which comprised of sections of various Shotokan kata, was always performed in true Enoeda style. Intense and dramatic, with the loudest of "kiais" that shook the very foundations of Crystal Palace. Then the sleeves would be hitched up and four adversaries

SAKURA   TOKAIDO

東海堂

The President of Tokaido and Directors of Sakura Trading Co
Invite You To Attend The Sakura Tokaido Taikai 1978

BRITAIN SOUTH V BRITAIN NORTH

KUMITE CONTEST FOR THE SAKURA TOKAIDO
CUP & OTHER PRIZES

each team is comprised of 5 Shotokan
and 5 Wado Ryu members
plus

DEMONSTRATIONS BY SENIOR MARTIAL ARTS
MASTERS INCLUDING SENSEI ENOEDA SUZUKI
HARADA &INSTRUCTORS IN AIKIDO & KENDO
SAKURA EQUIPMENT SHOP; FILM SHOWS &
EXHIBITS; RAFFLE FOR VALUABLE PRIZES

Enquiries
TO: SAKURA TRADING CO Tel 568 2152 &
560 8282 Mon-Sat 9am- 6pm

Tickets
FROM SAKURA BY POST OR FROM OUR
SHOP £2-50 each ORDER IMMEDIATELY AS
SEATING IS STRICTLY LIMITED

sakura

JOIN US AT CRYSTAL PALACE FOR OUR VERY
FIRST CHAMPIONSHIPS NEXT SEPTEMBER 16th
AT CRYSTAL PALACE NATIONAL SPORTS
CENTRE LONDON SE 19

Exhibition Opens 12 Noon Championship Starts 5-30

;Ticket Order Form Page 12

FRIENDSHIP TAIKAI
CRYSTAL PALACE NATIONAL SPORTS CENTRE
SEPTEMBER 16th TICKETS £2-50 FROM SAKURA T/C

would enter the area. Single, double and multiple attacks would ensue and Enoeda would dispense with ease all of his attackers to rapturous applause. It certainly was a great day out. The nationals were later moved to the National Indoor Arena in Birmingham after many years at Crystal Palace, but although the event was always very professionally organised, the atmosphere and excitement of Crystal Palace were never recreated at this venue, which always seemed to resemble a rather large and cold aircraft hangar.

Mrs Chieko Buck had a working relationship with Sensei Enoeda that started in 1977 and spanned 26 continuous years. Remembering her early working days she recalls, "I was looking for a part-time job as I was studying English Literature at that time. Mrs Tomita introduced me to Sensei Enoeda, as she knew he required a part-time secretary. When I went for my interview I climbed many flights of stairs to the top of the Marshall Street building for the first time. I was soon to get used to them – there was no lift!"

"When I met Sensei Enoeda I found him to be very smartly dressed and pleasant towards me, as he explained just what the job involved. He had a big strong voice, which gave me confidence in him. I thought, this is nice and easy, answer the telephone, take the training fees for the classes and still have plenty of time for my studies. I didn't have a chance to think about taking the job; Sensei wanted me to

start straight away! I worked from 5.30 to 8.30 in the evenings and soon found that there was no time to spare. My workload gradually grew to take in meetings, translation and attending to Sensei Enoeda's official and personal business with Europe and Japan."

I asked Mrs Buck what it was like to work for Sensei Enoeda. "It was hard work and sometimes very difficult and demanding, but I saw Sensei as a great karate man and a true family man. He was dedicated to his family and, like a good son, always looked after his father who was very proud of him. He was always very considerate towards his parents. If I ever needed to visit my mother in Japan, he would always say, "Go straightaway – please make sure you look after your mother." There was never any question of whether or not I should go. I was told to go straightaway and stay as long as I needed. I appreciated his consideration as I have an ageing mother living in Japan alone.

In the early nineties, Sensei Enoeda's father travelled to England from Japan to see his son and his family. He visited the Crystal Palace Course to watch the karate and was very proud to see just how successful his son Keinosuke had become.

There was always a daily stream of courses and gradings to be taken care of throughout the United Kingdom. As well as the many clubs that had to be visited, Sensei Enoeda made regular visits to Oxford and Cambridge Universities as well as the famous Eton College. There was a mutual feeling of respect between the students and Sensei Enoeda at these institutions, and there was also some enjoyable socialising when students were invited into the Enoeda household. He appreciated greatly these visits to various educational establishments, and liked to see the energy of youth that was evident during the classes that he took, which must have reminded him

Sensei Enoeda inspiring and teaching at the Red Triangle Dojo in Liverpool, 1968, with Bill Crystal in the front row

of his own early years at Takushoku University.

During his years resident in Great Britain, Sensei Enoeda continued to teach on large international seminars, courses and training camps. America, Africa, Russia, Algeria, Norway, Finland, Scotland, Nigeria, Greece, Germany, Italy, Sweden, Portugal, Spain, France, Barbados and Ireland were all visited each year, sometimes more than once His loyal assistant Mrs Chieko Buck was the organiser for these trips, arranging flights, arrivals and departures and scheduling much of the timetable for Sensei Enoeda's activities, including the twice-yearly Crystal Palace courses. Mrs Buck, or Chieko as she was always affectionately known, also dealt with a continuous stream of phone calls, faxes and other communications that were essential for the smooth running of the Enoeda itinerary throughout the year. Administration of the Marshall Street Dojo, which was functioning lunchtimes as well as evenings, was also a duty that Mrs Buck added to her workload. There was always a daily flow of new students who required membership, visiting students from other countries, plus the regular grading examinations and administration that was involved in running the dojo itself.

Throughout all of this, the demand for Enoeda worldwide was growing by the day. There were not many weeks during the year when his passport and bag were not packed and ready to fly. In fact the Enoeda passport which would last a normal traveller for five or ten years had to be replaced after just two years. The pages were full and there was no further room for the many visas that were required. The time differences in travelling to these various countries must have been very difficult to acclimatise to and so must have been the food and drink. Sensei Enoeda told me this story over a drink one evening. "In Africa I had to be very careful of the drinks, I could not drink the water and if I drank beer it could only be the imported type, the African beer upset my stomach. It was a dangerous country, even in the restaurants! At one restaurant I visited with some students in Gabon, the food was being served and an alligator slid in and started walking about! I jumped up and could not believe my eyes."

On 1st October 1985, Sensei Enoeda was awarded 8th Dan – Number 17, by the JKA in Tokyo.

JKA Dan Grades Awarded to Master Keinosuke Enoeda

Shodan – 1st Dan. 27th November 1955
JKA registration number 1,200

Nidan – 2nd Dan. 23rd November 1956
JKA registration number 333

Sandan – 3rd Dan. 13th June 1960
JKA registration number 150

Yondan – 4th Dan. 12th June 1962
JKA registration number 63

Godan – 5th Dan. 8th March 1964
JKA registration number 25

Rokudan – 6th Dan. 1st April 1970
JKA registration number 25

Shichidan – 7th Dan. 1st April 1974
JKA registration number 21

Hachidan – 8th Dan. 1st October 1985
JKA registration number 17

Kudan – 9th Dan. 29th March 2003
JKA registration number 8

The USA Connection

There was a tremendous demand for Sensei Enoeda from the United States of America, and for many years he travelled across the Atlantic as a guest instructor to the ISKF Master Camps held in Pennsylvania. The annual Master Camps were organised by Sensei Teruyuki Okazaki, and many of the world's top instructors were regularly in attendance. The list of names reads like a history book of karate: Okazaki, Mikami, Yaguchi, Koyama, Okomoto, Takashina, Suzuki, Ochi, Schmidt, who, together with Enoeda, were all regular or guest instructors on these courses. For many years Master Masatoshi Nakayama was a regular guest instructor in addition to Sensei Tanaka, Tabata, Osaka, Asai and Sugiura. The USA indeed had an insatiable appetite for the very best that Shotokan had to offer. These trips to the USA

The Pennsylvania Master Camp 1998, organised by Master Teruyuki Okazaki 9th Dan

completed the circle for Sensei Enoeda that was started in his early teenage years; Sensei Okazaki was the gifted and inspirational instructor who first caught the eye of the teenage Enoeda and inspired him to take up karate seriously at Takushoku University. That early meeting of the spirits had a profound effect on Enoeda as well as the hundreds and thousands of karate students throughout the world who have subsequently been influenced by him. It seems wonderful that the embryonic relationship with Master

Okazaki started so many years ago, developed and continued to grow in such a rewarding manner. Enoeda was undoubtedly well thought of in the USA. The students loved his uncompromising Samurai approach and as well as the karate training they also listened to his stories that were woven into the classes with the creative skill of a great teacher. His stories told in the same way all over the world, provided a measured counterpoint to his lessons, which were always intense and dynamic. Since his first early

excursions abroad, Sensei Enoeda always had close links with America. As well as travelling regularly to the USA to teach on courses, he also taught for some time in the 1960s at the dojo of Master Okazaki in Philadelphia, as well as the New York dojo which later became a base for Master Mori.

The ISKF news team ran a small interview with Sensei Enoeda at the end of the 1996 Master Camp. This interview took place after a full week of training with Master Enoeda. The interview went like this. "Enoeda Sensei's spirit is legendary and the enthusiasm he transfers to the class pushes one much further than most of us have gone before." And further on in the interview; "Sensei, in the final class you taught a very difficult combination of Jodan Age-Uke, pivot and Jodan Uchi-Mawashi-Geri. Do you train with those types of combinations in England?

Sensei – (breaks into laughing) – "That is a hard technique, isn't it? Very hard, very difficult to do correctly. Timing, balance, everything must be just right. No, I am not teaching these kinds of kicks in Europe. I did that today because this was the end of camp and I wanted people to leave with the knowledge that there is no limit to karate techniques."

"Sensei, you are famous for the spirit you display both inside and outside of the dojo. Is spirit something you develop, or are you born with it?" Sensei Enoeda replied. "I would say that it is a combination of both. As a child, I was high-spirited and enjoyed judo and kendo. It was not until Okazaki Sensei came to my high school and gave a karate demonstration that I realised that karate was exactly what I was looking for. As soon as I began training I was able to use my kendo and judo enthusiasm in an activity

Masters Koyama 7th Dan, Takashina 7th Dan, Schmidt 7th Dan, Enoeda 8th Dan, Yaguchi 8th Dan, Okazaki 9th Dan, Mikami 8th Dan and Sagara 8th Dan in the USA

that I enjoyed more than either one of the others. Spirit is very hard to define. I feel very fortunate to be able to practise every day. I always feel that I must honour my seniors and instructors by being a good example to the students. Just try your best every day no matter what you are doing."

The following year there were further examples of the effect that Enoeda was having upon students in the USA. Mr Rex Ingram who was at the time a 7th kyu student on the 1997 Master Camp, recollects an eventful class with Sensei Enoeda. "I was asked to write briefly about my experience at camp and specifically about the classes taught to beginners. There were only about twelve of us in the 10th kyu to 7th kyu classes compared to hundreds in the advanced classes. While training at the smaller hall by the lake, we would hear the thunderous sound of a hundred "kiai" echoing from across camp. Imagine a sea of movement among the black and brown belts compared to a few of us seated together listening to the soft-spoken voice of our instructor. It was not uncommon for some of the black belts to come down after finishing their class to watch our group training and to watch closely the instruction given to us. Because the instructors rotated, we had the same teachers as the advanced and intermediate classes. There was a sense of directness or accessibility to masters like Enoeda, Yaguchi and Koyama. Whilst we were training, Master Enoeda called me to the front of the group. I made my best front stance and just as he had done to the others previously, he toppled me with a slap to the shoulder. I remember thinking that his point was to show us the instability of front stance from any force applied to the side of the body. If this were true though, why did he look so disappointed each and every time one of us fell over? He allowed me another try, and I tried with all the strength in my legs to hold the stance but, again, he pushed me over rather easily. Unlike the others, he called me back a

third time, left leg forward, left arm and fist extended to Chudan level. He stood in front of me and pointed to my head and said, "Mind". He reached out and grabbed my yellow belt and said, "Body". He then took my fist in both of his hands and said, "This is your mind and body together....Focus." This time, when he slapped my right shoulder, I stayed upright. He slapped me harder the second time but, again, I didn't budge. One by one he brought the members of our group forward to focus and withstand his blows. That event may have been the most profound experience I had at camp during that year. It also revealed to me the depth and complexity of Shotokan Karate."

Douglas Walsh also explains the effect that Sensei Enoeda had on him in America and how he came to London to train with the "Tiger".

"I am an American 4th Dan student of Master Takayuki Mikami who knew Master Enoeda quite well. When I was training as a brown belt, I became aware of Master Enoeda from the old JKA kata videos (Bassai-Dai, Jitte etc) and also from his *Advanced Kata* books. I was totally impressed by these, and in the photos one could see and feel Master Enoeda's spirit."

"In November 1988 shortly after gaining Shodan, I made a trip to London, partly for music reasons but mainly to see the man who had inspired and impressed me so much with his karate. Upon reaching London, the first thing I did was go to Marshall Street. Master Enoeda was not there, but Ohta Sensei was. I just went to watch that night, and then returned again on Monday night. Upon reaching the top of the famous stairs, I heard a tremendous "kiai" and a loud voice. It seemed the whole building shook. It was then on November 21, 1988 that I got to see the "Tiger" for the first time. I was able to train with him several times in his dojo and found the experience at times quite intimidating. His students

**Sensei Enoeda with Mr. Douglas Walsh
in the USA**

were outstanding, as was the general etiquette of the dojo. One night I arrived late for class. As we all walked down the stairs after class, I said, "Sensei, I am sorry I was late for class." I guess he did not hear me. He stopped in his tracks looked up at me (I was right behind him) and said "Pardon?" I was scared for a moment! I then repeated myself slowly and he seemed to make me feel at ease saying, "Oh, it's OK." I remember him later at the local pub after training, jovial, laughing and talking with his students."

"I also attended his demonstration at the Royal Albert Hall on November 27, 1988. This was for a Martial Arts event that I believe was called the Budokwai, which featured judo, karate and the Royal Marines. It was truly an outstanding event. Master Enoeda gave a tremendous demonstration, dressed in Hakama, doing his own special kata and then his kata application. The lights and the music also added greatly to the demonstration as his "kiai" thundered throughout the Royal Albert Hall. I noticed a martial arts display in the one of the display cases in the Royal Albert Hall, which had a book called *The Martial Arts* by Peter Lewis, with Master Enoeda on the front cover. Whilst using the Underground tube train in London, I also clearly remember the poster adverts for the Marshall Street Club and Master Enoeda."

"One night as we left the Marshall Street Dojo I asked for a photo with him. "Not now! Must be in Dojo!" came the terse reply. Unfortunately it was my last chance to see him in London before I left to fly back home. I was sad, yet determined to see him again."

"During the summer of 1990 Sensei Enoeda was to visit the ISKF Master Camp at Pennsylvania. I was so excited to know he was coming to this camp. I knew I had to go. On a lunch break during the course whilst in the cafeteria, he was sitting where the Masters sat. I was walking through the cafeteria, he saw me and gestured towards me. I looked at him and pointed to myself saying silently, "Me?" He nodded his famous nod and so I approached him. "Where are you from?" he asked. I said, "New Orleans. I train with Mikami Sensei and trained with you in London at Marshall Street in 1988." "That's it, that's it!" he said and nodded. I was truly flattered he remembered me."

"One evening after training he was outside drinking a Miller beer whilst waiting for Yaguchi Sensei to go play golf. I approached him and during the conversation mentioned that I taught Mikami Sensei's Dojo youth class. He said, "Ah, very good!" Then after a pause, I said, "Sensei, you have been one of my biggest influences in Karate-Do." His face lit up as he smiled and then he tapped me lightly on the cheek and said, "Ah! Good boy!" "Of course, my own Sensei (Mikami Sensei) and others have all been tremendous influences as well, but having just finished an unbelievable class with him at that time and at that moment, I was in total awe of the man. There was something truly special about him. Later, on the last day of training, he taught another unbelievable class with some of the most tremendous combinations I have ever seen.

Then he talked to us about the "cat and mouse story" and about us using 110%. I remember he kept saying, "Use your STOMACH!" He signed books and had pictures taken too. I was so happy to get a photo with him. My photo with him was printed in John Cheetham's *Shotokan Karate* magazine published in August 1990, when I wrote a report about the ISKF Master Camp for the magazine. Talk about feel honoured! I'll cherish that for the rest of my life."

"I saw the great man again in ISKF Master Camp 1992. It was at this camp that I was honoured to demonstrate for him. I was in the back of the class and weaselled my way up to the front. I think he noticed this. While doing a kumite exercise, he called another guy and myself forward. We both later became friends. I think this was due to the moment we shared doing that kumite exercise up front in the dojo. I felt there were few times previous in my training when I tried so hard. At that point Master Enoeda was explaining control. "You MUST use control!" He then demonstrated his tremendous control and power on me. I was never injured, yet felt safe as a baby in his parents' arms."

Sensei Enoeda with Sensei Takashina and Mr Douglas Walsh

"I saw him previously in Master Camp 1997 when I first attempted my Instructor and Examiner test. He was also grading some people trying for 4th Dan. At one point he called them up to the table and asked loudly "You not practice Tekki kata?" The candidates seem scared to death. Mikami Sensei then said more quietly, "He asked if you ever practice Tekki Kata."

"He also was in the area where I was testing for my 'C' level Judge. He kept calling me and the other judges over and asking why I was calling a conference with the other judges. He told me not to do this. I later passed 'C' Judge at our National Tournament. I remember he spotted someone videoing once his class! He stopped and yelled "Oi !!" and shook his head and hand towards the camera. He yelled for Takashina Sensei to tell the person not to video. Takashina Sensei then made sure the student left the area. He was at Master Camp again in 1998 the year I tested for and passed my 'D' level Instructor and 'D' level Examiner. I did not attend in 1999, but heard a true story. While teaching a class of intermediate students, he was walking around the class. Someone mumbled something. It may have been a non-English speaker who did not understand what to do. Master Enoeda stopped and asked the student, "What did you say?" The student replied "Nothing." Immediately, Enoeda Sensei told him to leave the class!

"The last year I saw Master Enoeda was in 2000 at ISKF Master Camp. I remember being in one of his classes and having the honour to say the Dojo Kun in Japanese. I said it loud, proudly knowing who was at the front of the class. Later that day I was walking up a driveway as Sensei was walking to a class. I told him I wanted to go see him in London and told him I was a musician. He said, "Oh, you musician, that's why you like London." I replied, "I want to go to London to see you Sensei!" He laughed and said, "Oh, good, good!" I told him I had no accommodations and knew no one there. He said, "Before you come, please contact me, I find you a place." I said, "Osu! Thank you Sensei!" Sadly, that

Sensei Enoeda officiating in the USA

never happened. I live with the regret that I did not see him one last time. Especially in London at Crystal Palace. Life is too short. Who would have known? I have lots of photos with Master Enoeda and every book I have of his is signed by him. I have lots of magazines that are also signed by him. I treasure them all, but mostly, I have great memories of him. Not only did he influence my karate, but also my attitude and outlook on life. He will always be in my heart."

Karate students and instructors from all thirteen ISKF regions in the United States descended upon Hawaii in November 2003 for the 26th National Championships. The event was huge and was dedicated to the memory of Sensei Enoeda. Master Okazaki gave a stirring tribute on behalf of the entire organisation with his fine words. "Mr Enoeda was an important part of our ISKF family. He was here at the Masters Camp for many years and he taught at our headquarters dojo in Philadelphia for one year. He was a good instructor, a good ambassador for karate. We will miss him very much."

Sensei Harry Tagomori Ph.D. is the regional instructor for the Hawaii region in the USA and his contact with Sensei Enoeda over many years had a profound effect on him. "Keinosuke Enoeda Sensei visited Hawaii annually in January. This was his retreat and vacation. On two of his many visits, he taught the students of the Pacific Shotokan Karate-Do (PSK). It was a very good experience for the students, who had the opportunity to train under a JKA master. The

atmosphere was different from the usual PSK classes. It seemed more intense. Everyone who trained with Enoeda Sensei at the University of Hawaii Dojo and the main Dojo at the Japan Cultural Center of Hawaii remembers him as a brilliant teacher. We were saddened by the news of his passing."

"Early in my karate endeavors, I was not familiar with Enoeda Sensei except for information in publications and from other instructors. My personal library included several of his works and my impression was of a person who was very strong and someone every karateka would like to emulate. I learned that his nickname was "Tora" because of his fierce competitive style. I wanted to meet him in person. My wish came true when I met Enoeda Sensei for the first time while at instructors' training in San Diego in 1977. He, like all the JKA instructors I trained under, gave me inspiration to train hard and learn more about the art of karate. When the training ended, I never thought I would ever see him again."

"In 1999, I started the PSK (Pacific Shotokan Karate-Do) youth division. Through this division, I met Mr Noboru Kobayashi, chief instructor for the JKA, Chiba Prefecture. Through Kobayashi Sensei, I met Enoeda Sensei again, although he didn't remember me from instructors' training camp in San Diego. Our meeting this time was more casual, and I had the pleasure of sipping sake and talking with him. He joked with my daughter, Dara, as we all relaxed at Mr Kobayashi's estate in Honolulu. I had the pleasure of meeting Enoeda Sensei again in January 2001. As usual he was happy to teach students of the PSK. After class, I took him back to the hotel where he was staying. I will never forget that night. On our way to his hotel, he put his hand on my shoulder and said, "You are my friend." I didn't know what to say except nod my head and smile. I felt honored that such a distinguished teacher would say that to me. At the entrance of the hotel, we got out of the car and paid our respects to Enoeda Sensei. After we shook hands, he turned and gave my daughter a big hug."

"It never occurred to me that this would be our last meeting and that I would never see him again. In the moments that I have had the honor of associating with Enoeda Sensei, I gained a new dimension of karate-do and the true meaning of trust and loyalty. He made me feel proud to be a member of the Japan Karate Association and the International Shotokan Karate Federation."

The 2004 ISKF Master Camp and Good Will Tournament at Pennsylvania was also dedicated to Sensei Enoeda – the ISKF's way of saying that he will be missed, but never forgotten. During an interview to discuss the event, Master Okazaki gave tribute. "Master Enoeda was a member of our family. He came to America many times to teach at our camp and by doing so, with his special leadership qualities, he helped our members develop as karate-ka and as people. It is important to me and I know it means a great deal to our members as well, to have this year's ISKF Master Camp in honour of Master Enoeda."

The 1992 Pennsylvania Masters Camp. Sensei Enoeda and Ochi were special guest instructors, together with Sensei Okazaki, Mikami, Yaguchi, Koyama and Takashina

Marshall Street

A NYONE IN THE VICINITY of Marshall Street baths in London on a Monday, Wednesday or Friday could be forgiven for looking shocked and suprised at the sounds that they heard. The spirited "kiais" from the students many floors above in the dojo would echo and reverberate around the tourist areas below. The effect was even more eerie at night when the streets were less crowded.

Inside the Marshall Street Dojo

The Marshall Street Leisure Centre

I am a beginner in karate and have been training for maybe three or four months once or twice a week. The club that I regularly attended has closed down, the church hall left empty, the instructor decamped abroad. It was sudden. There was no willing student or instructor to take over this sad and unwanted spectacle and it is only now that I realise that I like karate, I like the discipline, the struggle and the challenge. I want to continue.

This is why I have found myself in London's West End at the heart of the tourist area in Carnaby Street, with visitors posing and cameras flashing. I am searching for and successfully find Marshall Street Baths, an ancient ten-storey building, much older than most of the other glitzy and neon-illuminated buildings and establishments in the area.

I enter the building and attempt the challenge of the one hundred steps that lead to the top floor and the karate dojo, high above the ground floor swimming pool. I reach the last of the foot-worn stone stairs glad of the polished brass handrail that lends support from the bottom to the top of this powerful Victorian building. The bag carrying my karate uniform seems heavier now than it ever did before. It is 11.00am and the repetitive rhythmic crash I heard faintly on entering the building has now become a deafening jungle-like banging every two seconds. Reverberating through the building, the sound draws me closer as a tribal drum might call an ancient village to order. I pass through a small red-carpeted reception area. Relics and trophies of past battles arresting my eyes. A Union Jack and a Japanese Rising Sun flag greet my nervous arrival together with a centre-piece framed picture of a Japanese Master I have only ever seen in books and magazines before. I shouldn't be here. This place seems almost religious and yet I am drawn towards the sound. Close now, I turn the corner of the reception area and see the most wonderful, traditional Japanese karate dojo, a

The Marshall Street dojo poster

The Marshall Street dojo

golden glow from the bright wooden floor reflecting the new day's sun.

Master Enoeda himself in his pure white karate gi is facing the wall in a forward stance, punching and attacking the Makiwara with a frightening force that I heard one hundred steps below. I silently watch,

The souvenir display cabinet

transfixed by the spectacle. There is only him and myself present. He does not know I am here. If he does, he ignores me, and the piston that is his arm continues to drive into the upright padded post, which he is punishing with his reverse punches. For a further five minutes, the punches continue. The hypnotic rhythm roots me to the spot. I see the sweat running down the side of his face as the uncaring sun washes down through the part-glazed roof and I wonder how I was brought here.

The last punch echoes around the dojo and then there is silence. Master Enoeda relaxes and shakes off the sweat. Still not appearing to notice me, he walks to the far end of the dojo. There are two pictures on the wall, both I have seen before in books and magazines. One pictures him kicking and one punching. Techniques that in my few weeks of practise, I am not familiar with. I recognise the dojo code printed on two boards adjacent to the pictures. The sun is like a furnace now and I am mesmerized, unable to speak, watching something that seems deeply personal and religious.

Master Enoeda is reverently adjusting parts of a small Shinto shrine that is affixed to the wall at

Sensei Enoeda

the far end of the dojo; the same wall as the pictures, the dojo code, and a large scroll of Japanese calligraphy, which covers a fire exit door. The special white paper parts of the shrine are being adjusted and moved back into their proper position. He does this with a quietness and reverence that one may see of a priest in a church. He takes a step back and stands with his feet together seeming to nod his invisible approval at the shrine and the adjustment that he has made.

He turns and begins to walk towards me – slow and confident, this is his ground. His bare feet pad lightly across the shimmering floor and for the first time, I see his face full on, exactly like the pictures in the books and magazines. Carved like a statue of a Samurai Warrior with hair as black as jet. I automatically move to the side as he bows and exits the dojo area. I bow and give what I know as the usual karate greeting, "Oss, Sensei". Master Enoeda grunts "Hai, Oss" and enters the small office adjacent to the dojo.

Still nervous, I wonder if I should go, if this is really the place for me, a mere white belt beginner. Too late, I cannot escape. Master Enoeda's face appears through a small open window in the wall of the office. "You want karate?" His voice is loud and frightening. "Oss, Sensei." "You a member?" the voice returns almost shouting. "No, Sensei." I explain the demise of my karate club and the predicament I am now in, and Sensei Enoeda says

The class in action

The class begins

simply: "You train here!" "Oss, Sensei", I reply. I feel excitement of the unknown and an empty sickness in the lower part of my stomach as with my hand shaking, I carefully complete the membership form and pay my dues.

I am directed to the changing room and find other students now also there in the process of donning their white karate uniforms. Some are talking, but I know no one. I secretly tell myself to follow their actions to make sure that I adhere to the correct form and etiquette that is required and essential in every karate dojo. One by one we bow and enter the dojo area, twelve of us in all, nine men and three ladies. We move to the sidewalls and bow as Sensei Enoeda enters the dojo. I know I must find a position in the lines of students that is not senior to my beginner's rank. I am quickly moved into place by one

of the senior black belts, and the class begins.

We kneel and bow to Sensei Enoeda, the warming up is short, about two minutes, but luckily my joints are already lubricated and made loose by my nervous and premature sweat. Gedan Bari… Oi Zuki … Jodan and Chudan up and back, over and over. Then Age Uke, Ude Uke, Uchi Uke, forward and back. "Faster, stronger" came the command. Then facing each other, Sanbon Kumite or Three Step Sparring, everyone fired up and ready for mortal combat. To count and then no count. "Change partners." Repeat again and again. I must block these punches, which seem to be getting nearer and more dangerous. My head is dizzy, the sweat is in my eyes and I am seeing double, but I must continue, I must be faster and stronger. Then just at the point of collapse, I hear "Yamae – line up." "Everyone lie down." Backs had to be off the floor whilst we did one hundred punches and then one hundred front snap kicks. "Stand up." Mae Geri forward and back many times. "Yamae! Kihon Kata", came the command. To count, then no count full speed. The volume and tone of his voice driving us onwards beyond the point of collapse. At this point my mind detached itself from my body, I seemed to be lighter and faster than ever before. I felt stronger, as though I could keep going forever, nothing could stop me. My karate suit was now like a second skin, welded to my body and soaked with sweat. An innermost store of power that I have never experienced before surged through me like an electric current charging every cell in my body. Finally, we knelt, recited the dojo code and performed the final bow. Everyone moved to the sidewalls and bowed again as Sensei left the dojo. I noticed the clock on the wall – 12.30pm! The class had lasted just 30 minutes. I received a welcome smile from one or two of my sparring partners and I know this is where I want to be. This is karate!

Many years have passed since that first incredible meeting with Sensei Enoeda, and I have sweated many gallons over the years in the same Marshall Street Dojo, which is now sadly closed. Thousands of people have passed in and through the entrance of the dojo and there have been countless visitors from overseas who wished to train and pay homage to the "Tiger of Shotokan Karate". I have made many long-term friends through training at Marshall Street and there have been some incredible experiences and very exciting times. Some of the members were training regularly at Marshall Street for 25 or even 30 years. My good friend Harry Wilson was amongst the longest standing members. Tony Lacey, Jim Kelly, Sue Waughman, Robert Richards, Craig Raye, Roy Tomlin, Gary Stewart, Lupcho Apyepski, Pauline and Ray Fuller and Dave Hazzard also trained under Sensei Enoeda for many years at the dojo. Elwyn Hall was there for quite a few years and the sessions were always adrenalin-packed when this top international was training there in the class.

David Hewson was one of the very first members of the Marshall Street Dojo and started there after training with Sensei Enoeda at the Budokwai, and at the Blackfriars Dojo, which Sensei Enoeda began when he first arrived in London.

Says Hewson: "I and other members helped put the wooden dojo floor down in the Marshall Street Dojo. We also walked around Soho pasting up adverts on street corners for the club. Sensei Enoeda was somebody who I believe respected not only the high fliers in karate but also those of us who made the effort to achieve our full potential. He was a great leader and motivator of people and inspired all those who came into contact with him."

This must have been an extremely exciting time for Sensei Enoeda, and the arrival of a young and gifted JKA Karate Instructor from Japan created even more excitement for the students of Sensei Enoeda in London.

Sensei Enoeda in action

Sensei Tomita performing Yoko Tobi Geri

The Arrival of Sensei Tomita

I met Sensei Hideo Tomita and his wife Terumi at Utsuwa-No-Yakata, the fine china store in the Oriental City shopping mall at Colindale, North London, where Sensei Tomita's business is based. The meeting was to gain further insight into the working relationship and the friendship between Sensei

An early Marshall Street class with Sensei Tomita

Tomita and Sensei Enoeda. Sensei Tomita was there in the early days of Marshall Street and the Crystal Palace courses and these were the subjects that I was interested in. We had coffee and lunch and I enjoyed greatly talking to and listening to Sensei Tomita who is held in high regard by many practising karateka.

Sensei Tomita was Sensei Enoeda's assistant in the UK for ten years teaching on a daily basis at Marshall Street and previously at the Budokwai and Blackfriars dojos. He also travelled extensively in the UK and taught on special courses with Sensei Enoeda during weekends.

It was obvious right from the beginning that Sensei Tomita regarded Sensei Enoeda as his teacher and he was the student. "I learnt so much from Sensei Enoeda about

Anyone for tennis?

Playing Mah Jong on the beach in Spain

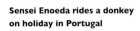

Sensei Enoeda rides a donkey on holiday in Portugal

A relaxing family holiday in Turkey

karate, techniques and teaching skills. I learnt to analyse and explore the techniques of karate." A great teacher and communicator himself, I discovered that there was much more than the kohai, sempai (student, master) relationship involved inside and outside of the karate dojo. Sensei Tomita was the vehicle to take Sensei Enoeda away from the pressures, politics and problems that being the chief instructor of the KUGB and chief instructor of the JKA Europe involved. Sensei Tomita is entirely without any political agenda and this must have been truly refreshing for Sensei Enoeda who was the subject of many invisible pressures from the KUGB and the JKA.

Sensei Enoeda escaped these pressures for short periods of time with his family and Sensei Tomita's family. Holidays, golf and games of mah-jong formed a great release from the day-to-day pressures that Sensei Enoeda endured. "Sensei Enoeda taught me to enjoy life",

emphasised Sensei Tomita. "He also taught me to play golf but I was never very good. He was very patient with me and encouraged me, but I was not a good player."

During these times the subject of karate was carefully steered away from and Sensei Tomita was extremely perceptive in helping Sensei Enoeda to escape for these short periods of time. Sensei Enoeda found a man that he could relate to in terms of fun, enjoyment and communication. Sensei Tomita realised this and nurtured these times sensing the difficulties that his teacher experienced. He and Sensei Enoeda laughed, ate, drank and played together outside of their time teaching karate. Travels and holidays abroad were a great way to get away from the pressures of the karate world as was the regular socialising with games of mah-jong. (Mah-jong is an ancient Chinese game of skill using a board and small bricks similar to dominos in size.) The Tomita and Enoeda families continued to enjoy these holidays and times together long after Sensei Tomita ceased being a full time karate instructor.

Sensei Enoeda king of the waves, floating in the Dead Sea

The memories of these times are particularly precious to Sensei Tomita. He recalls their 2001 holiday at Killarney in Ireland, where there were many enjoyable games of golf. He also recalls the last year's 2002 holiday together in Turkey. "The accommodation, food and environment were excellent. We planned to return there, but it was not to be."

Behind these regular social diversions that Sensei Enoeda enjoyed, Tomita was also the backbone for Enoeda's karate activities in the UK for no less than ten years. The relationship started in Japan, at the JKA Honbu during 1968/1969. Master Takagi introduced the pair, as he knew Tomita was interested in visiting England.

Marshall Street students on the beach in Spain

"Sensei Enoeda was very friendly towards me and after saving up I made a three week holiday trip to England. I helped briefly at the Budokwai intending to return to England later for one year to learn English. Sensei Enoeda suggested two years would be better and he invited me to stay and help and see how we got on together. I was happy and moved over permanently in 1972."

"At that time it was quite difficult to make a living from teaching karate but then something happened. The Bruce Lee films started to be shown everywhere. Although the films were basically kung

Sensei Enoeda demonstrates on Sensei Tomita

fu, many people became interested and keen to practice all martial arts including karate. I remember one day at the Marshall Street dojo there were so many students packed in that they overflowed out of the dojo and onto the carpet in the reception area. We could only do punches and kicks on the spot; there was no area or space to move forwards or backwards! The Bruce Lee films encouraged two kinds of people to start karate. Some left when the training became too difficult, but some liked the spirit and concentration and decided to continue. These people stayed at Marshall Street for many years."

These were early days for karate in London, and gradually Sensei Enoeda's teaching activities were focused more on the new Marshall Street dojo and away from the Budokwai and Blackfriars dojos. These two dojos continued and were looked after by other instructors. John Anderson kept the Budokwai dojo running successfully for quite some time. Seymour Hall in London's West End was also used as a dojo for a while before Marshall Street started. The first KUGB Southern area championships were held in Seymour Hall, but local residents complained to Westminster council about the noise, particularly the "kiais". The complaints were actually a blessing in disguise because that was the point when the council finally offered to Sensei Enoeda a permanent base in Marshall Street Leisure Centre.

Sensei Enoeda travelled regularly back and forth to Japan each year to see his family and to get back to his roots at the JKA Honbu. On the 1st of April 1970 he was awarded his 6th Dan, with 25 as his JKA registration number once again.

This time coincided with the arrival of Tomita, the beginning of the Bruce Lee period and the opening of the new Marshall Street dojo. The dojo, which started functioning in 1973, soon became extremely successful, riding on the wave of popularity that the martial arts and particularly karate were beginning

Sensei Kon, Kawazoe, Enoeda and Tomita at the 1977 Christmas party in the dojo. Chris Herrington and Jim Kelly are behind

Sensei Tomita in fine voice

to enjoy. "The classes were packed. There were Marshall Street parties and training holidays abroad. We travelled with students to Spain and Greece for karate holidays which were great fun and very enjoyable. The parties in Marshall Street were the only time anyone was permitted to wear shoes in the dojo, including me!" laughed Sensei Tomita, who then without any prompting gave testimony to the power of the Enoeda punch. "In the early days we did displays and exhibitions of karate around the country often involving some quite dangerous techniques. On one occasion Sensei Enoeda did some tile breaking, punching through a large pile of roofing tiles. Although I have seen tile breaking, I have never ever witnessed anything like this before. A hole was punched completely through the pile of tiles; Sensei Enoeda's fist had travelled through the tiles at such speed that a round hole was left in the centre of the pile of tiles. Normally the tiles just shatter into many pieces, but this tile breaking was completely unique. I have never seen anything like that before or since that day."

Jim Kelly, one of the students of Marshall Street at this time, has some wonderful recollections of the holidays abroad. "We have many fantastic memories from when we went on SKC holidays abroad. In the earlier years the amazing Sensei

After training on the sand

Tomita joined us on holiday, and his legendary contribution to the development of Shotokan throughout the UK is immeasurable. We used to have to be up and on a Spanish beach by around 5.00am most mornings, training. This was a forum where all our inadequacies certainly came to light. Basic limitations of ability and possibly what we were up to just three or four hours earlier were the culprits. We had a Kata-Star in the club called Sue Waughman and without her the beach-experience thing would have been even more daunting. Sue was the only one who could think straight at that time of the morning. However one morning during the kata Kanku-Sho, Sue fell down a big dip in the sand (it was still pitch black at the time). Yes, you guessed it, in our absent mindedness we all followed her rather novel move! Every morning Sensei Enoeda was always so eager, so energetic, and full of life, we had no option but to bluff our way through. Sand gets everywhere you know."

"On one occasion, when training was suspended, we were on an early morning ferry taking us from

Sensei Enoeda demonstrating

At home in the dojo

Gyaku zuki punch, Enoeda style

**An evening out together: Mr And Mrs Enoeda,
Mr And Mrs Kawazoe and Mr And Mrs Tomita**

the Greek mainland on an island-hopping excursion for the day. Breakfast on board was Metaxa brandy! Sensei Enoeda went to great lengths to point out to us that this was a very ancient Japanese tradition not known to many people, and was only handed down through generations of Samurai and then only if your first name begins with a "K". So who were we to argue? We grudgingly partook of this traditional brandy-breakfast. The breakfast was so good that we later started betting on the silliest of things. We were sitting in a bar opposite a large mirror located by the entrance. Sensei decided that we should turn our betting attention to whether the next person to come through the door would look in the mirror at himself or herself, or not. The losers of each bet would have to buy and replenish our traditional breakfast feast. Yes, how cool was that, really adult behaviour, well, it did keep us out of trouble for a while until our next training session."

"At the end of each torturous, and alcohol shrouded early morning training session on the beach, Sensei Enoeda would instruct us all to line up behind him, in total silence. While the small rippling waves would be lapping at our feet, we would be taking deep breaths and meditating, looking out to sea at the beauty of the rising sun, as depicted on the Shotokan emblem. This was to have an everlasting effect on me and would become a poignant and eternal memory. I now live on high ground to the west of London in Buckinghamshire, where fortunately, I experience many exquisite sunrises. This is the time I see my friend, Keinosuke Enoeda, and the time I reflect on how lucky I am to have known such a man."

"To this day, with great nostalgic pride, I can still see his unique aura and presence, silhouetted against the golden sun that majestically rises from whence he came: the East."

During these early years in the UK there were many other JKA instructors who assisted Sensei Enoeda and helped karate to grow in popularity. Master Kanazawa who was the first JKA chief instructor in England had left to return to Japan. Sensei Enoeda carried on in 1968 where Kanazawa left off as the JKA chief instructor. Sensei Hideto Matsui assisted greatly in the early days when Sensei Enoeda first arrived in Liverpool. Sensei Shiro Asano from Takushoku University was an old colleague of Sensei Enoeda who covered most of the central region and now has his own organisation, SKIGB. Sensei Kato assisted with karate activities throughout England and also helped with one of the first books by Enoeda. He now runs his own Kodokai organisation. Master Kawazoe came over to stay in England from Madagascar and helped greatly with Sensei Enoeda's teaching responsibilities in the KUGB, at Marshall Street and also on the early Crystal Palace courses. He also now runs his own organisation. Sensei Hashiguchi also assisted for some time during the 1980s when Sensei Ohta who arrived in 1982 was later away in Japan.

From 1972 onwards Sensei Tomita was teaching full power and full time for Sensei Enoeda. The pressures of teaching caught up with him quickly, and Sensei Tomita recalls: "I learnt so much from Sensei Enoeda but if I felt unwell I could not take a day off. One day I had flu with a very high temperature but I still had to travel and teach the karate classes. I am from a different generation to Sensei Enoeda. His generation had a very strong instinct for survival.

After the War food, work and money were difficult to come by in Japan and so the generation spawned by these times became very strong and determined. Sensei Enoeda would just keep going and I had to do the same. I had to practice my karate before and after the lessons that I took, to continually improve and find my own body technique." Sensei Tomita stressed this point a few times. "Everyone is different in build, size, weight and power; I was encouraged to watch and copy, but find my own personal body technique myself. Sometimes my body would ache and be stiff but these were times I would stretch, do some more karate and then feel better."

Sensei Tomita has been a regular guest instructor on the Crystal Palace courses for thirty years now. He explains many of the finer points of karate technique in great detail with his tremendous grasp of the intricacies of the English language. He continues with his very successful family business, Utsuwa-No-Yakata, based in Colindale, north London, and now also assists with the JKA England courses and gradings throughout Great Britain which are organised by Sensei Ohta.

Sensei Tomita was a loyal and trusted friend to Sensei Enoeda, who also taught on the September 2003 memorial course held at Crystal Palace in honour of Sensei Enoeda.

The Enoeda and Tomita families together, on holiday in Spain and in London

The Arrival of Sensei Ohta

Sensei Enoeda's reputation in Japan is enormous. On travelling to the Honbu in Tokyo with a letter or a licence signed with the Enoeda signature, the response is one of great respect, kindness, admiration and even envy. That one is lucky enough to be a student of Sensei Enoeda is enough to open many doors and initiate many questions. Every student and instructor in Japan knows of Master Enoeda. His reputation is held in total reverence. Yoshinobu Ohta, direct from the JKA instructor's class, held Master Enoeda with the same esteem as all of his fellow instructors and students and it was a feeling of nervous trepidation that accompanied him all the

way from Tokyo to Heathrow airport in 1982. In Japan he always held Sensei Enoeda in awe, but even more so upon his arrival in England.

Before the arrival of Sensei Ohta, Sensei Enoeda spoke to the members of the Marshall Street dojo explaining his reasons for the choice of Sensei Ohta as an assistant instructor. "He has very good technique, also good character and a very nice nature." He had obviously given his choice some wise and considerable thought.

Sensei Ohta arrived at Heathrow Airport from Japan on 11th September 1982. He flew over with Sensei Kon who at that time was also going to assist

The trophy display cabinet

with some of the teaching responsibilities in the United Kingdom. Who was waiting at the airport to greet them? Sensei Enoeda, of course! The incredible relationship, which started on that day, was to last for twenty years and develop to form one of the most enduring partnerships ever in karate. Ohta provided the counterpoint for the samurai spirit of Enoeda, with his challenging footwork and his brilliant technical innovation and expertise. A couple of years later, in 1986, he flew back to Japan to take part in the All Japan Championships. He returned to England after taking third place in the kata finals. He gained this position by performing "Unsu", one of the most technically demanding kata. Humble as always, he commented, "I was a champion for one day, now I have to train like a champion every day!" The trophy stood in the display cabinet at the Marshall Street dojo from that day onwards as an inspiration for many to achieve their full potential.

Sensei Ohta remembers those days twenty years ago very clearly. "I arrived in London on the 11th September and the very next morning at 7.00am I was training at Sensei Enoeda's house. I did that training every morning, seven days a week, without fail for three months, 7.00am every morning. We would run by the river or the road and then do kihon and kata in front of the house on the driveway. After three months, I found accommodation at West Norwood and just did the morning training with Sensei Enoeda on Tuesdays and Thursdays. I had to get up at 5.00am to travel and be ready for training at 7.00am. Before

I came to England the JKA also made me do lots of extra training. I was young, keen and very excited. Sensei Enoeda was regarded as a god in Japan; he was looked upon as being higher than a normal teacher or instructor. I felt very privileged to be in this position."

"I loved every second of this time and enjoyed the excitement of everything new. I found Sensei to be intense and dynamic. He led by example and just expected me to follow. I regarded him as my teacher and gradually learnt about his strong attitude and personality. I found that if I needed to ask a difficult or awkward question it was best to do this when I was driving and Sensei Enoeda was the passenger. That way I was not facing him, so it was much easier!"

"Outside of the dojo, we didn't talk much about karate. We both attended Takushoku University in our teenage years and so often we would talk about our days at university and about things that had happened there since Sensei Enoeda graduated. Karate was Sensei Enoeda's life – his personality. People loved to follow him. In many ways that was his philosophy; just follow or don't follow!"

For the first few weeks of his arrival, Sensei Ohta trained with all of the other students of Marshall Street whilst Sensei Enoeda was teaching, staying at the back of the class and encouraging students to push harder or "kiai" more. This is much the same as in the JKA Honbu; the seniors encourage the rest of the class whilst training themselves at the rear of the dojo. He gradually started teaching at Marshall Street and on courses in his own inimitable way. The dexterity of his footwork and the inventiveness of his classes was something that few had ever seen or experienced. Sensei Ohta took these skills to new peaks and for twenty years was one of the most popular instructors in the United Kingdom and on the Crystal Palace courses.

"For the first ten years with Sensei Enoeda I was mainly teaching in the United Kingdom, on courses and at Crystal Palace. During the second ten years I went abroad more, mainly in Europe to Norway and Germany."

Sensei Ohta worked diligently for over twenty years for Sensei Enoeda and has now assumed the cloak of JKA England and is the new Chief Instructor. Don't expect his skills and progress to stop or slow down!

Jim Kelly, one of the original students who trained at the Marshall Street dojo, commented on the abilities of Sensei Ohta together with the work and support of Mrs Buck. "Sensei Ohta is arguably the most supremely talented, highly revered and universally popular Sensei in karate today. He is the perfect person to continue Sensei Enoeda's dream of promoting this wonderful martial art at the highest level. Mrs Chieko Buck has been, and still is, the anchor, who loyally and super-efficiently keeps it all together. Chieko is a true unsung heroine in our eyes."

Jim, who is now a JKA 4th Dan, remembers his initiation into the Marshall Street dojo and his first meeting with Sensei Enoeda. He was at that time a green belt, graded by Sensei Yatou in Mexico. "I left Mexico in the very early 70s proudly clutching my grading book showing a 6th kyu Shotokan Karate pass. My sensei in Mexico was Sensei Yatou and he asked where I was going: I told him back to London. He wrote on a piece of paper in Japanese and said that this was an introduction to a fellow Shotokan instructor, it was of course, the Shotokan Tiger, Sensei Enoeda."

"So after re-settlement in London after further travelling, I plucked up the courage to pay a visit to the SKC Dojo, Marshall Street, London in early 1973. After passing the initial challenge of climbing what seemed to be an endless spiral of stairs, I arrived at the top of this echoic chasm where I heard the awesome sound of the Shotokan "Spirit", resounding all around me."

"On approaching the office, Sensei Enoeda was sitting, head down, class finished, counting with his abacus. I waited until he had finished; he lifted his head and looked straight at me. I was momentarily stunned and lost for words and I knew then that this was the great man himself. After regaining my composure, I gingerly introduced myself and handed him the introductory letter from Sensei Yatou. It was in Japanese and I had no idea of what it said. With very little reaction he stood up. With the combination of his own physical height and his powerful presence factor, he looked down on me from what seemed like his lofty twelve foot tall position and said something like: "You have Gi?" Shakily I said that I had; he growled, "Join next class!"

"Little did I know that in the fullness of time and almost thirty years later, this incredible man would remain my Sensei and, in my eyes, eventually become a valued friend. This familiar presumption is not intended to overstep any Shotokan ethics; scores of us felt we had developed a "special relationship" with this master of karate. He contributed so very much to the quality of not only my life, but also to thousands of others."

I am convinced that Jim had a unique relationship with Sensei Enoeda that was rare. The jokes and banter between them both are legendary. Who else could get away with saying in a rather threatening manner, "Be careful or I will take you outside!", to

Sensei Enoeda? At that point Sensei Enoeda would say, "Oss, Jim, I very scared". The banter would go on and on like this for some time and onlookers could be forgiven for looking somewhat nervous. Jim explained his close friendship with Sensei Enoeda: "Sensei Enoeda, apart from being a larger than life character who enjoyed life to the full, was armed with a very British sense of humour and was a warm, caring and sensitive family man. Occasionally we would enjoy private and often intimate conversations, as if between two friends. Every time we spoke it came across to me in no uncertain terms, that his priority was always for the happiness and well being of his family. The Enoeda family home was always called "Sunrise". I became one of the SKC "oldies" and therefore was summoned to join the SKC committee, which is a gathering of Karateka who helped with the running of the club and organising of the competitions. On many occasions we would be invited to Mr & Mrs Enoeda's beautiful houses in Teddington or Esher, for a committee party. We were spoilt by wonderful Japanese hospitality and traditional food, and we all knew what a great privilege it was for us to be invited into our Sensei's family home and to meet his wonderful family. One day Harry Wilson and myself pulled up outside Sensei's house and, as pathetic as it sounds, we actually felt sorry for the makiwara that was being pummelled by Sensei Enoeda in his garage. We often wonder what a structural survey of the garage would reveal. We have a pretty good idea! I have met many great friends during my involvement with the SKC, many are mentioned in this book and are part of Shotokan's extended family. The editor is indeed one of those."

The Marshall Street dojo itself was in a way two separate dojos. There were lunchtime sessions three times per week on Mondays, Wednesdays and Fridays, and evening sessions running from 6.30pm on the same days. Many of the students who were

Lunchtime students trained in their dinner break and often worked close by, hardly having any contact with the students of the evening classes. Most of these students travelled home in the evening before the evening sessions began. The Evening students, likewise, were not around during the day to train at lunchtimes, and their training was generally restricted to evening sessions. There were a few who had the luxury of taking both lunchtime and evening sessions; these were the very lucky ones. If Sensei Enoeda was away and there was no assistant instructor to take the classes, the senior students would have to help out and teach at the dojo. Jim Kelly, Jim Lewis, Roy Tomlin or myself would all take turns in teaching responsibilities during the lunchtime sessions. Sue Waughman, Robert Richards, Craig Raye or Lupcho Apyepski would look after the evening sessions.

There were regular Marshall Street squad training sessions, which helped to create and mould the ladies' and men's teams that went on to win the KUGB nationals and Southern region championships many times over. Sensei Enoeda pushed these squad members to their limits, instilling in them the indomitable spirit that he himself brought over from Japan decades previously. There were some brilliant competitors spawned from this squad training. Sue Waughman, Roy Tomlin, Gary Stewart, Craig Raye, Robert Richards, Elwyn Hall, Roy Cudjoe, Hassan Moussaoui, Barrie and Roy Watkiss, the list is endless. Many of these members also went on to become top internationals. I spoke to Paul Herbert who was one of the younger Marshall Street squad members. Paul travelled to Europe with the squad and was in many of the winning

Celebrating European success in Holland

The 2003 KUGB Nationals winning team: Darren Hamilton, Paul Herbert, Aissai Adjadj and Alex Stern

teams in Great Britain for the KUGB championships, and in Europe for the JKA championships. Each year Sensei Enoeda formed JKA England teams and travelled with the teams to the JKA European Championships. Belgium 1996, Germany 1997, France 1998, Czech Republic 1999, Holland 2000 and Finland 2001. Paul travelled to many of these events over a nine-year period and brought home many trophies during this time. He felt very honoured to take part in these events and had some wonderful recollections of his times in the squad and with Sensei Enoeda. "Sensei was always so proud of all of us. He was like a mentor, pushing us in the right direction, instilling a strong attitude and the spirit to win. When I first started training at Marshall Street he seemed like a legendary figure out of a book. I was so nervous whenever he spoke to me; he asked me where I lived. I thought he would never have heard of Bexley, so I said, "Dover, Sensei". It was the first place that came into my mind and for many years he thought I lived in Dover! It became a standing joke: "How is Dover?", followed by fits of laughter. The squad training at Marshall Street was very hard. In one of my first sessions I was so tired fighting Robert Richards I could barely stand. I put my chin out so that I would get hit, I could then have a rest. After the match Robert told me that he was doing the same thing! Sensei knew our limits better than we ourselves knew them. He wanted that fighting spirit from us and was not satisfied until he got it."

Paul was also in the team that won 2003 KUGB nationals. This winning contest was dedicated to the memory of Sensei Enoeda. Paul recalls: "When we walked out onto the mat we saw a large picture of Sensei facing the competition area. We knew we must win — for him — not for ourselves. We could almost hear him saying, "Just one more!". I was fighting third in our team. I wanted this pressure. In the previous years team final, I lost to Randy Williams and felt responsible for our whole team losing. I nearly cried. Sensei came close and said, "It's OK, don't worry". I learnt an awful lot from losing that match in 2002. This year was different and special, I wanted to feel the pressure and rise above it. We won the first match, lost the second and won the third. Winning this third match was a personal achievement for me, but most of all we won the 2003 Nationals for Sensei Enoeda and were very proud of that fact. I don't think anyone could have beaten us on that day."

The annual SKC (Marshall Street) Christmas Party was an event that everyone looked forward to greatly. Usually held on the first Monday in December, the party was hosted in various venues throughout London's West End during the life of the club. For the first few years the Christmas parties were held in the dojo and in 1979, Quaglino's Hotel became the venue. It is hard to believe that £2.50 or just $4 paid for the food and entertainment in this top class London hotel. During many subsequent years the famous Café Royal in Regent Street was host to this event, with top quality food, music and entertainment. It would be an evening to "dress up" in the smart black clothes usually reserved for this kind of special event. Sensei Enoeda would cherish this evening, which was always very professionally organised by the previously mentioned, long time member Jim Kelly. Jim made sure that every detail was perfect. Music and clapping would herald Sensei Enoeda's entrance to the Green Room with his wife, Reiko, and many of their closest family and friends. There would always be a four-course meal, and Jim, who has a background in the music and entertainment business, would often travel around the tables whilst coffee was being served, performing entertaining magical tricks. Jim, being a singer and musician, also played saxophone and sung during the evening's entertainment, but as the evening went on and the meal was finished, it became time for Sensei Enoeda's speech and his eagerly awaited vocal contribution.

Jim explained with great humour some of the background to the singing and entertainment. "Ever the one for some fun, Sensei Enoeda used to team up with me in a torturous, annual Christmas ritual; where long suffering SKC members and their guests were subjected to both of us singing to them during our Christmas Parties. The best one must have been when I had to try to find the backing track of *Love Is A Many Splendoured Thing* for him. Would you believe I ended up giving Sensei Enoeda private lessons? Hold on, alas, they were only singing lessons. We focused mainly on his hugely successful album that I am sure everybody is familiar with: *Enoeda's Greatest Hits (and Kicks!)*. The finished result was certainly something well…um, momentous to say the least. He sang it in English, honestly, or so he said! It certainly was a splendiferous rendition! I would put it on a par to my own feeble attempts of Enpi!"

"I was led to believe by Sensei Ohta, that karaoke roughly translates means "empty hall". That word

Happy times at the dojo Christmas parties

takes me back to around 1979 when I was first introduced to something called karaoke. In his ever generous manner, Sensei Enoeda took a few of us to a very exclusive Japanese club, just off Regent Street in London. It was a far cry from what we would all recognise as a karaoke venue of today. The set up not only included backing tracks but also a brilliant pianist who you could try and sing with. Needless to say, Sensei had us up, one at a time, to entertain everybody. A short while afterwards I made a scheduled visit to Japan. Whilst there I investigated this phenomenon and brought back loads of tapes and promptly introduced karaoke into my business (Event Productions). Clients wondered what I was on about when trying to offer them karaoke. They said it would never take off in this country. It didn't, did it?"

After listening to Jim talking about these times many years ago, it occured to me that Sensei Enoeda might have been innocently and indirectly responsible for the introduction of traditional Japanese karaoke to Great Britain during the 1970s! We can debate whether or not this is a desirable import from Japan, but it certainly has become extremely successful.

As well as the music, Sensei Enoeda's speech would always be eagerly anticipated. The speech would be drafted out beforehand, and Sensei Enoeda would deliver it in his own inimitable way, barely needing the microphone to transmit his powerful voice around the Green Room of the Café Royal. After the speech a tape was played as a backing track for the traditional after dinner vocal delights. Occasionally

The first Christmas party at Quaglino's, in London's West End

the Frank Sinatra hit *My Way* would be sung, but *Love is a many Spendoured Thing* was always top of the pops in the Enoeda songbook. *Love is a many Splendoured Thing* was a song that Sensei Enoeda learnt in the 60s whilst in South Africa.

Shotokan Karate Centre
invites you to its
1979 CHRISTMAS PARTY
to be held from 8.00 p.m. on Monday, 26th November, 1979
in the St. James Suite of Quaglino's Hotel,
Bury Street, London, SW1
TICKETS £2.50 EACH
BUFFET REFRESHMENTS

The reason he learnt this song was to assist him with his learning and understanding of the English language. He was advised that singing would help greatly with his ability to learn English. He never lost his attraction for this song, and each year his voice would boom out the words at the SKC Christmas party to the delight of all present. I wonder what it first sounded like when he first started singing it in South Africa to learn English? The song always went down well and everybody enjoyed this traditionally Japanese part of the evening, which always finished with an enormous Enoeda smile and a rapturous round of applause from the audience.

One of the worst experiences I had to unfortunately share with Sensei Enoeda was at the annual Marshall Street Christmas party. I was the new chairman of the club; an honour bestowed upon me by some of the senior club instructors and committee members. The chairman had to make a speech and introduce the various sections of the evening to the many guests. These introductions included the speech and vocal contribution from Sensei Enoeda. His speech and the song were an integral part of the evening and always took place at a certain time. I got it wrong and didn't call Sensei up at the correct point. He was angry. He refused to make his speech. He sat down next to his wife Reiko, arms folded, whilst the whole party sat waiting. He wouldn't budge. I pleaded with him to make the speech. "No! That's it! I not do it now!" I could do nothing to make him

give his speech and song. Suddenly, Mrs Enoeda, who had been listening to this conversation for some time, whacked him on the arm and said, "Don't be so stupid, get up and make your speech." Like a lamb, he went to the microphone, gave his speech and went on to sing *Love is a Many Splendoured Thing* in his own very special way. I think I realised then that Mrs Enoeda "wore the trousers".

Jim Kelly was a great impersonator, and his impersonation of Sensei Enoeda was spot on. If he could be coerced into performing this impersonation, Sensei Enoeda would always be extremely amused; the likeness, voice and mannerisms were exact. In later years Erich Pich and Sue Sinclair, instructors from the Kilburn clubs, also did Christmas impersonations in costume that were hilarious. Sensei Enoeda always saw the funny side of these light hearted jokes and acts performed at his expense, and would be rolling up with laughter together with everyone else.

I knew Sensei Enoeda and trained with him for a relatively short period of time, just twenty years or so. However, in the years that I did get to know him I was "volunteered" to assist with many small and insignificant responsibilities. One of these responsibilities was to write the speech that he gave each year at the Marshall Street annual Christmas Party. I took over this responsibility from Jim Kelly who was the previous chairman of the Marshall Street SKC committee. Sensei would give me a broad idea of what he would like to say and I would get it written down in a clear and concise way, adding in a few "Christmas trimmings". I suppose because of this, I had hoped he would approve of and enjoy reading this book, which was actually started in 1993 with a few taped interviews and notes that I made.

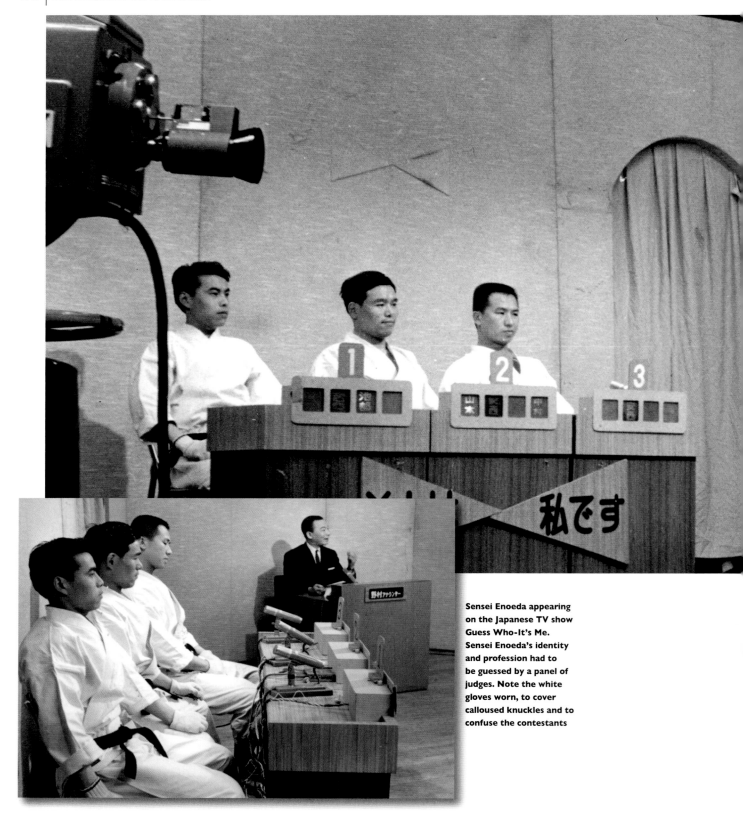

私です

Sensei Enoeda appearing on the Japanese TV show **Guess Who-It's Me.** Sensei Enoeda's identity and profession had to be guessed by a panel of judges. Note the white gloves worn, to cover calloused knuckles and to confuse the contestants

Something we all attempted to do at the Marshall Street dojo was to seek his approval and prove we were indeed worthy of that approval.

Each year during the Christmas and New Year holiday the dojo had to be redecorated. A team of us would be dressed in overalls and then wash the dojo and changing rooms from top to bottom before repainting the walls and ceilings with fresh white paint. This was a tradition that went on each and every year. As well as making the dojo look clean and smart, I understood from Sensei Enoeda that it

was also a good way to get rid of any "bad spirit" left over from the old year. We would always be treated to a nice meal and a Christmas drink afterwards and the chore always seemed more like fun than hard work. There would also be a Christmas party at the Enoeda household. Sensei's wife Reiko would lay out a wonderful spread of Japanese food and drinks. A karaoke machine together with lyrics on a TV screen would ensure everyone had a go at the traditional Japanese singsong. Mrs Enoeda was a truly fantastic hostess creating a spread of wonderful Japanese delicacies. This ensured that the music, eating and drinking and fun went on until the early hours of the morning.

One of his many great gifts was to make everyone feel special. He could do this to a white belt who had just started karate or an experienced 4th or 5th dan karate instructor. His Marshall Street classes would be bursting with intense encouragement, so much so that you believed you could achieve much more than previously. I am sure that everyone who has trained in his classes or on his courses has experienced the following scenario. While working on a kumite drill, the attacker has to step forward with Mawashi Geri. The defender has to shift back, block the kick and spin round countering with Ushiro Mawashi Geri – Jodan! To most of us mere mortals, this is an extremely difficult manoeuvre, however with Sensei Enoeda standing behind you shouting "Jodan", the foot flies up and your partner gets a nice tweak of the ear! Previously this technique seemed impossible, but not with the magic of Sensei Enoeda behind you.

He could likewise do this kind of thing with speed, making you go faster and faster. I remember as probably many others do, being in one of his classes and doing some basic combinations. We had been working non-stop for about 10 minutes on these basics. It was hot and there was a lot of sweat on the floor. Everyone was giving their all to the point of exhaustion. "No, faster!" shouted Sensei Enoeda, and from somewhere that extra bit of speed and kime was delivered. Again, he took you further than you thought it was possible to go.

Marshall Street Baths in London's West End was the home of Shotokan Karate in London. This was Sensei Enoeda's dojo and while he was based there, students arrived weekly, from just about every country in the world to train, pay their own respects to the "Tiger" and obtain a little bit of that magic I mentioned earlier. The hundred steps leading from the ground floor up to the dojo reception area were worn thin by the feet of thousands of karate students.

One very strange visitor arrived towards the end of one of the lunchtime sessions. He stood in the middle of the dojo entrance and said in a very loud voice that he wanted to fight Sensei Enoeda! We all thought this must be a madman. As the class finished, Sensei Enoeda bowed and left the dojo area. The man, who actually looked perfectly normal, was standing in front of Sensei Enoeda's path. He was brushed aside and knocked flying as Sensei Enoeda walked "straight through" him. Two of the senior members moved swiftly over and escorted the man downstairs and away from the building. He must have been crazy; he certainly was not drunk. We never saw him again.

There were club gradings at the Marshall Street dojo held regularly every three months. Everyone would help with the paperwork, calling the names and distributing the coloured belts at the end of the grading. Sensei Ohta would give the commands for the examinees, and Sensei Enoeda would mark the grading records. Towards the end of one particular grading, two brown belts were attempting their 2nd Kyu examination. When it came to the kumite section of the grading, the defender was blocking and hitting his opponent rather hard on the face with his counter-attack. Sensei Ohta shouted "Control!". The student continued to block and hit his opponent again. At this point Sensei Enoeda shouted "CONTROL!". The kumite continued, and once again the offending student hit his attacker, this time knocking him down. Sensei Enoeda rose from his seat shouting "You STUPID! – I told you CONTROL!". He was told in no uncertain terms to leave and I seem to remember this person's licence either being torn up or thrown out of the window! This event was an exception to the normal format of the Marshall Street gradings, where many students from all over London would attend if they didn't have a club grading of their own. Usually when the grading was over and the students had dispersed, we would all head for the Japan Centre or another Japanese restaurant for a good hot meal.

I came to enjoy many meals out with Sensei Enoeda, often in Japanese restaurants or sushi bars. The first experience of this happened in Finchley, North London. We were hungry after having completed some chore during the evening. We were travelling along the Finchley Road, when he said: "We eat sushi, I have a friend who owns a restaurant here". We stopped at the restaurant, entered and there was a very warm welcome from the proprietor whom Sensei Enoeda had not seen for some time. We started eating sushi, lots of it! In fact we kept

Like a Japanese Peter Pan, karate master Enoeda has defied the advancing years to teach his martial art to generations of Londoners. **David Hurst** meets the man who taught his father to get a kick out of life

chopaholic

DYNAMIC KARATE

The Evening Standard article

A Christmas party with family and friends at the Enoeda home

eating and eating and ordering more and more. We were eating with our fingers, as we were so hungry. Eventually the sushi chef declared we could not eat any more, all the rice was gone! We had cleared a whole basin full of rice with our sushi feast and complained in a lighthearted way that we were still hungry. The proprietor apologised that there was no more sushi and bought out two enormous deserts. Of course we had to eat these so as not to appear rude or ungrateful. We were in fact quite full.

On another occasion, Sensei Enoeda had ordered fish for a meal. The whole, rather large fish appeared on a plate in front of him, head and tail intact and a rather large eye looking up at him. He looked at the fish, deep in thought, with a serious expression on his face. He suddenly picked up a spoon, scooped out the eye of the fish and, turning to Jim Kelly, said, "Jim, EAT! Fish eye very good for karate, make you see in the dark and see behind you who is coming!". Jim took the spoon and had to eat the fish eye. Sensei Enoeda almost fell off of his chair laughing! He was unpredictable, with a sometimes evil sense of humour and this humour often seemed to distinguish itself at meal times. After a long grading examination, a group of us once took him for a meal. All the meals had arrived on the table except Sensei Enoeda's. We were all waiting until his meal arrived before we started. Without any warning he turned to my partner Lucy who was sitting next to him, suddenly grabbed a fork, and started eating her meal! He was laughing and we all took this to mean we should start eating. Meal times were always fun when Sensei Enoeda was there.

The annual Club Championships were held towards the end of every year and all members were encouraged to take part. There was kata and kumite for ladies and the same for men. The team event would be lunchtime students against the evening students and there would usually be three or five competitors in each team. The seniors had to do the judging and refereeing for all of the events. Sensei Enoeda would sit at his table watching, keeping score and making sure that none of the officials made any mistakes. During one of the men's individual events there was a rather unfortunate incident. Two brown belts were fighting in the kumite event. There was a clash and one of the students went down. He was clearly in a lot of pain and his whole arm and shoulder was hanging loosely and looked as though it was about to become detached from his body. He had completely dislocated his shoulder. Sensei Enoeda ran over and instructed two of us to hold him in position sitting on the floor whilst he relocated the shoulder. We held him firmly. Sensei lifted, pulled and tried to push the arm and shoulder back into position while the student was screaming out in agony. There was a grinding, scraping sound as Sensei tried again to get the shoulder back into place. Eventually it clicked back into position with a rather loud noise. The student stopped screaming, got up and the match continued. We were all stunned into silence.

Trophies and medals would always be awarded to the successful finalists. At the end of the Championships each year Sensei Enoeda would elect one of the seniors in the club to present the trophies. The Enoeda sense of humour ran through all of his relationships with his senior students and instructors. This year was no different. Harry Wilson was to present the trophies to the male and female finalists. Harry started the presentations and then Sensei's voice boomed out. "No, Harry! You are doing it wrong! You must kiss the ladies when you present the trophies!" Harry duly obliged with a big smile on

his face. Then Sensei's voice boomed out again. "No, Harry! You are still doing it wrong! You must now kiss the men too!" At this point Harry's nerves got the better of him, he wasn't sure if this was some kind of strange tradition, a serious request, or one of the Enoeda jokes.

Most of us would have small jobs that we did to help with the smooth running of the dojo. One of the jobs that I undertook was to make a display of all of the front covers of the karate magazines that Sensei Enoeda appeared on. There were a great number of these and I thought they might look good framed and hung around the reception area of the dojo at Marshall Street. They were all subsequently framed by Robert Richards, and I then fixed them into place on the joists around the reception area. I told Sensei Enoeda, who was in his office, that the job was done and would he like to have a look. I heard him shout my name: "Rod – what have you been doing? You have all these to do yet!" And then he came out of the dojo office with another pile of karate magazines from around the world. Needless to say, there was not room on the walls for all of these front covers!

The karate press loved him. He made great pictures and in many ways was a celebrity of the Martial Arts press all over the world. In 1998 the Marshall Street Dojo had been in operation for 25 years. The *Evening Standard*, London's daily newspaper, celebrated this fact with a full one-page article and photograph which were seen by just about everyone in and around London. Posters advertising club details together with a picture of the famous Mawashi Geri were a common sight on London's Underground rail network. The *Evening Standard* article featured a reproduction of this famous Marshall Street dojo poster, which seemed to become almost iconic in its presence all around London. *The Times* published an obituary notice and picture, and over the years I have collected other articles that have been published

in the press, as well as all the other martial arts publications.

He has also been in films and TV adverts and appeared on TV chat shows and game shows in Japan and in the UK. He was very proud of his celebrity links and had worked with Sean Connery, Michael Caine, Ingrid Pitt, Lee Marvin, Peter Sellers and

Sensei Ohta, chosen by Sensei Enoeda for his technique, skill and personality

Edward Fox, over the years acting with them and coaching them in their fight scenes. Sensei Enoeda also appeared in the James Bond film *You Only Live Twice,* and understandably Sean Connery (James Bond) is probably the only person to ever put him down and beat him in a fight scene; such are the skills of actors and moviemakers. The film, released in 1967 was a tremendous success and is rated as the best one ever by most of the knowledgeable James Bond critics. The action for *You only Live Twice* took place in Japan and also featured Japanese stars Mie Hama, Tetsuo Tamba and Akiko Wakabayashi.

Ingrid Pitt, the actress, was also a long time student of Sensei Enoeda and regularly attended the Nationals while they were held at Crystal Palace. For many years, pictures of Sensei Enoeda with various celebrities hung in the Marshall Street office and reception area. The largest was a picture of him with Lee Marvin, but there was also a very good portrait of him with his family sitting with Margaret Thatcher.

There were five years of negotiations and discussions with Westminster Council about the impending closure of Marshall Street due to redevelopment of the site. Being protected by the Tenancy Act, there were rights that had to be considered and in fact the karate club stayed in the building long after all of the other various clubs and businesses had gone.

Marshall Street Sports and Leisure Centre, however, after years of procrastinating by Westminster Council over modernisation and redevelopment, finally closed down on Friday 29th September 2000. We moved everything out of the dojo and a few of us took part in one last symbolic lunchtime session with Sensei Ohta from 12.30 to 1.30pm and one last evening session with Sensei Enoeda from 6.30 to 7.30pm. We all had a drink in the dojo afterwards, but it was a drink of remorse, which tasted sour, the smiles were forced and hard to come by. It was an extremely sad time for both classes. Students from Marshall Street subsequently continued their training at the Oasis Sports Centre in Holborn with lunchtime sessions, the Budokwai in Kensington with evening sessions and for some time the 3rd Space Fitness Centre in Oxford Circus. The Oasis and Budokwai clubs still continue to this day, now under the guidance of Sensei Ohta. Sensei Enoeda together with Sensei Ohta tried for one year to keep the 3rd Space club going, but it was price restrictive to students because of its very expensive central location and so it eventually closed down. This must have been an extremely difficult time for Sensei Enoeda and a very sad day on 29th September 2000, to see the long, almost 30-year history of the Marshall Street dojo come to an end.

The last lunchtime session at Marshall Street with Sensei Ohta

Crystal Palace

THE CRYSTAL PALACE COURSES organised by Sensei Enoeda were like an institution, a giant magnet that drew students and instructors from all four corners of the world to London twice a year, for the ultimate in karate training.

Crystal Palace was synonymous with the Enoeda courses

The original Crystal Palace was an impressive structure built of iron and glass and erected by William Paxton in Hyde Park to house the great exhibition of 1850. In the following year the building was moved to the present location where it stayed until 1936, when it was completely destroyed by fire. The site lay derelict until 1951 when an act of Parliament was passed to develop the site for the purpose of education and recreation and for furtherance of commerce, arts and history. Sir Gerald Barry proposed the building of the National Sports Centre. Work started in 1960 and the centre was completed in 1964 at a cost of £2,750,000. After just 40 years it seems as though Crystal Palace has reached the end of its useful life as a sporting venue

and a world karate venue. Ironic that the venue has had a life span almost exactly that of the Enoeda era 1963–2003.

For 35 years the cream of JKA instructors and All Japan champions travelled over to London to instruct on the courses. Over the years participants on the courses travelled regularly from the USA, Africa, Israel, Norway, Germany, Scotland, Ireland, Sweden, Spain, Portugal and many other countries. Some countries sent large contingencies of karateka, and most of these stayed in the lodge, the tall ten-story building adjacent to the Crystal Palace sports centre where breakfast, lunch and dinner were served. There was small but comfortable accommodation here, with beds that welcomed weary limbs. Students

The Crystal Palace main sports hall

The Lodge and the party room

who attended each and every year looked forward to renewing many old friendships and it was these longstanding international friendships that gave the courses an extra dimension of enjoyment.

This was Sensei Enoeda's European JKA course, open to all grades and organisations. The annual courses began in 1967 and originally took place twice per year, for two weeks in the spring and another two weeks in the summer. Times were later amended to one week in the spring and one week in the summer. For the last few years, the two courses ran for just four days during the bank holiday in May and four days including the bank holiday in August. I remember in the 80s attempting to do the whole two weeks of the course (most students sensibly only attempted one week). I survived the first week, but by halfway through the second week

The lower entrance to the Crystal Palace sports hall

The 1989 May
course poster

I could hardly stand up. My leg muscles had locked up and my feet had become raw with the friction of the floor.

There were also gradings for kyu and dan during the course, and it was quite easy to see in advance just who was to be taking dan grading. There would be a silent mental concentration outside of the dojo by the candidate together with diligent extra practise before and after the classes within the dojo. Sensei Enoeda would be in charge of these gradings and if he didn't like a student's technique, attitude or control, he would simply throw the relevant license and documents onto the floor. Subsequently, a candidate often knew before the results were given if he had passed the grading or failed! Sometimes during the kumite part of a grading, his finger would point and his voice would boom out "CONTROL!". He definitely did not like people using powerful techniques with little or no control. He liked and wanted GOOD karate. If he thought a student could do better, he would keep him fighting for a little longer to give him a chance. "Just one more", is the phrase so often heard when he wanted that extra little bit of power from someone whom he thought could do better. If he didn't like a candidate's kata, he would ask, "Who taught you that?" Most of us who were instructors with students taking the grading, dreaded

The famous Enoeda signature

The Enoeda karate display watched by Sensei Kase and Shirai

Right: a young Terry O'Neill together with the Japanese visiting instructors watch the Enoeda display

this question being asked for obvious reasons. Finally, the names would be called out by one of the helpers, and the words that all of the 1st Kyu students wanted to hear would be heard even in the furthest reaches of Crystal Palace. "PASS SHODAN." The famous Enoeda signature was usually hand written on the successful candidate's licence and this would be proudly scrutinised after the grading. This signature used to really have an effect on the young children who had taken a dan grading. They would run to their parents, faces moon-shaped with joy and relief, showing off their licence with the Sensei Enoeda signature, not quite believing that they were going to shortly be wearing a black belt.

For many years the KUGB National Championships were held on the Saturday that fell in-between the original two weeks of the course. Many competitors would travel from all over Great Britain to London for a week's training at Crystal Palace, before competing on Saturday in the Nationals. This was also the day that Sensei Enoeda performed his unique and renowned karate display. Before the final events of

the evening the audience would be seated, the lights would dim. Japanese music from a distant time would echo around the Crystal Palace sports hall packed to capacity; from the loud speaker system a deep and resonant voice would set the atmosphere even further. Words of ancient Samurai warrior battles and victories would pin the spectators to their seats, and the tension would rise. Spotlights dramatically illuminated the central area of the main arena, and Sensei Enoeda would stride forward and enter. To thunderous applause and dressed in his long and flowing black hakama, he would perform his own unique kata. The kata was created from many of the Shotokan kata that are regularly practised and to my knowledge, Sensei Enoeda would never teach this kata in any of his classes. One would recognise a series of techniques from one kata, but then there would be a seamless change into another kata and then another. Flowing in all directions, kicks and punches would fly out from the black hakama like arrows and swords against an invisible enemy and the "kiai" that finally finished the kata lead the audience into more thunderous applause. The upper part of the black hakama would then be quickly tied into place to give space for further manoeuvre, and four would-be assailants would then enter the arena, one from each corner. Each in turn would attack Enoeda with full power and be subsequently blocked, swept

At Heathrow airport Master Nakayama and the Japanese instructors from Takushoku University are welcomed by their hosts

or thrown in all directions. Then there would be multiple attacks and the bodies would be unceremoniously thrown, dropped to the floor and finished off with extreme realism. Over the years many assailants would be volunteered for this job and I remember one extremely powerful senior member of this team admitting to and showing his nerves in no uncertain way hours before the event.

Cyril Cummins, a long-standing veteran of the Crystal Palace courses, attended each and every one of them over the thirty-five year period. The first in 1967 included Kanazawa, Takahashi and Asano as well as Enoeda. Cyril particularly remembers the 1968 courses with Ochi, Miyazaki, Sumi, Kase, Shirai and

A day to be remembered. Masters Nakayama, Enoeda, Kawazoe, Tomita and Naito line up for the formalities of introduction

Sensei Enoeda with long-standing course attendees Rosemary and Arthur Hall

any twenty-year-old. Rosemary and Arthur attended all of the Crystal Palace courses over many years apart from one, which was due to sickness.

Just about every top instructor from the JKA in Japan visited and taught at Crystal Palace. Nakayama, Osaka, Tanaka, Mori, Ueki, Tabata, Yahara, Tsuyama, Kawazoe, Imamura, Ogura, Tomita, Ohta and countless others all brought their own individual styles and techniques to Crystal Palace, which were eagerly devoured by the hundreds of visiting students each year. The spinning back fists and in the air techniques of Yahara. Who could ever forget his rendition and application of UNSU, when he seemed to stop in the air six feet off the ground whilst defending against two attackers. The bunny hop repetitions and intensity of Tanaka; the dark look in his eyes froze even the toughest to the spot. The throws and takedowns of Kase, with his low centre of gravity, he gave kata techniques an even more profound meaning. The machine gun punches of the late Sensei Tabata, who smiled whilst we attempted his one hundred punch combinations, his voice building up in speed and volume like a giant steam engine reaching full power. The technical information imparted by Osaka while

even Master Masatoshi Nakayama who performed a wonderful demonstration of kata. Master Nakayama demonstrated the kata "Sochin" and its application of techniques with Sensei Osaka. Sochin became the hallmark of Sensei Osaka who for many years won kata championship titles with this, his favourite kata.

Rosemary and Arthur Hall were well known to everyone on the courses and regularly travelled all the way down from Nottingham twice per year to train with Sensei Enoeda and the Japanese visiting instructors. This wonderful couple who are perhaps a few years older than the average course participant, typified the friendship and camaraderie that was one of the main ingredients on the courses. Known to just about all of the regular course goers, Rosemary and Arthur would update old friendships, while news and information was eagerly exchanged. Then they would get "stuck into" the karate just as eagerly as

The 1989 and 1990 Crystal Palace course posters

The Crystal Palace courses attracted hundreds
of karateka from all over the world

Kawazoe, Miyazaki, Enoeda and Tomita share a joke outside

we watched his Sochin performed to perfection. The beauty of Ohta's technical skills and his complex and challenging footwork, all etched in the memory of those who took part.

Sensei Enoeda always regarded Mori as his senior and he would always be placed in the most senior position in the line up. Another graduate of Takushoku University (graduating in 1955), Sensei Mori bought a sense of tradition and history to the courses. Everything had to be correct. The standing position, the bowing, the lining up; anything less than perfect was not acceptable.

I remember spending a long time in one of the classes whilst Sensei Mori admonished us all for lining

Sensei Ohta, Ueki, Mori, Enoeda and Tomita pose with students for a group photo

up incorrectly, he then instructed the whole group of black belts on how to line up and bow in the correct manner. He would change the positions of the line up constantly to check everyone's technique, taking time to put us all right. Many who had less than perfect etiquette found Sensei Mori's classes difficult and hard to understand,, but many loved the tradition, discipline and skill that he brought directly from the early history of the JKA.

Students would arrive early in the main sports hall to register their attendance and loosen up. Sensei Enoeda was always there, talking to the other visiting instructors or doing his own pre-lesson warm up. He was supple and even in his 60s he would be able to drop down into full box splits and lean forward, chest on the floor during his own personal warm up. "Line up," came the command and the large sports hall, packed to the brim would have maybe ten or fifteen lines of students stretching across the full width of the enormous hall. Ohta would take a good ten or fifteen minute warm up and then the whole course would be split into separate groups – black belts in one group, brown belts in another, purple, green, yellow, red, orange and white belts would be in another two or three separate groups. Each instructor would take one group and there would be a volunteer in each group to assist with any translation or interpretation that was required.

Enoeda himself bought something to the Crystal Palace courses that no one else ever could or did. When he was present, you knew that something special was going to happen – and it usually did! You were taken from your usual maybe slightly comfortable position into a world where you perform faster, stronger and more focused than ever before. A performance enhancing drug is how it is best described, albeit perfectly legal and with no bad side effects, other than your whole body aching from head to toe the following day. When his lesson started the

Although disciplined and intense, there was always a joke to be had at the Crystal Palace courses

adrenalin would be pumping full power straightaway; I remember in the early years of the courses there would be injuries early on in the morning, where students who were not ready for this intensity of training lost control of their power and techniques. The first class of the day always included kihon and kumite and the second, always kata with perhaps some application of kata techniques. This was the general running order for the classes, which never seemed to vary except for the last day of each course. This last day I personally enjoyed greatly. Sensei Enoeda would take us through each and every kata that had been studied on the course, maybe eight or ten in all. We would work through all of the katas in plenty of time with "deep breeding" (deep breathing) and stretching throughout the class. It seemed as though we had all survived a kind of initiation ritual at Crystal Palace and there was always a wonderful relaxed feeling on this last day of the course. At this time Sensei Enoeda was

Sensei Tomita, Tsuyama, Enoeda, Kon and Kawazoe together with the late Sensei Hayakawa

Training outside at Crystal Palace

always very relaxed and happy and he seemed to cherish each of the katas that we revised. At the end of training on this last day, students would queue for autographs and photographs of the instructors. Over the years there must have been thousands of photographs taken in the giant Crystal Palace sports hall.

Training in the main Crystal Palace sport hall.

On a sunny day Enoeda's voice would boom out and rattle the rafters of the great Crystal Palace hall "All outside!" he would shout. We would leave the main hall and spill out onto the adjacent sports field for training, a reservoir of white on the warm green grass. These days were perfect. Usually we would enjoy kata with kata application in the afternoon outside and it was truly great to train in the open air on the grass on a beautiful summer day. Sensei Enoeda loved training outside and wherever he was in the world, he always took the opportunity to train outside if it was at all possible. I remember on one occasion all of the males on the course were allowed to take their gi jackets off and train in just gi bottoms whilst we were outside on the grass. The trousers of my male partner were getting lower and lower. He suddenly became the object

of attention of Sensei Enoeda and some of the ladies on the course. He had to quickly stop and redo his attire before becoming the star attraction of the day.

Lunch for many of us, if not staying in the lodge, would often be a picnic on the grass, the wet with sweat gis hanging on the branches of nearby trees to dry. The branches of these same trees are now unreachable; such has been the growth of the trunks and branches during the subsequent years of the Crystal Palace courses. During these early one and two week courses, there would be a long lunch break from 12.00 to 3.30pm during which plenty of food

Sensei Tomita, Enoeda, Kase, Shirai and Kawazoe

and liquid was, and indeed needed to be, consumed. There was time also for note taking – the comments and teachings of each instructor were carefully noted down for future reference. I have books of these notes and enjoy checking back to see what was done on some of the early courses. I developed a kind of shorthand so that I could write down quickly what we had been doing in each of the classes. For example, GB OZJ means Gedan Barai, Oi Zuki Jodan. KZ MG GZC means Kizami Zuki, Mae Geri, Gyaku Zuki Chudan. I have of course developed this kind of shorthand further and still use it today to make notes. It proved invaluable at Crystal Palace when many things had to be remembered and taken into account during one's daily training.

The children or junior members on the courses would often receive a special treat from Sensei Enoeda. A treat, not of the material kind but just as enjoyable. He would sit them all down in a circle around him, maybe ten or twenty of them and tell them a story. These stories usually imparted some kind of hidden message to the children in order to help them in their understanding of life and of their karate. One of those juniors who is now an adult and at work remembers the "old cat" story from his childhood. *"An old lady living in her house was troubled by a very naughty mouse that kept running around and taking her food. She decided to get herself a cat to get rid of the mouse. The cat was too old. It just lay there on the floor looking at the mouse. The old lady decided to get a younger cat to catch the mouse. All day the younger cat ran around chasing the mouse. It didn't catch it. The mouse just laughed. The older cat just lay there looking and watching. When the young cat got tired, it lay down out of breath and went to sleep. The mouse came out to see what was happening. As the mouse came out, the older cat that was waiting jumped and caught the mouse in one swift movement. The old lady was very pleased with the clever old cat."*

Sensei Enoeda explained that "Sometimes it is best not to rush around and be impatient. It is often better to wait a little longer and take your time."

Another story went something like this. *"A very old lady lived alone in her house a long, long time ago. She kept all of her money, life savings and jewellery in a big suitcase underneath her bed. The suitcase could not*

Mike Gardner, one of the course organisers, entertains with his Rocky Horror Show and Mrs Mopp impressions

The children and even some adults would sit around Sensei Enoeda mesmerised by these tales, his face telling as much of the story as his words. Sometimes whilst Sensei Enoeda was struggling to find the correct word to use, the story would be momentarily suspended in space, and mouths would be open waiting for the key to the tale. The eyes of the listeners would be wide as the story slowly unfolded before them. He certainly was a good storyteller, holding in suspense their attention right until the end of the tale. In a way these stories regularly dispensed to the children, were just as important as the karate training itself. At the end of the story the karate class would resume with added enthusiasm and spirit. Sensei Enoeda had got what he wanted. At the finish of each class there would be spontaneous applause from each group that was being taught and the lines of students would then reform facing the front of the large dojo, to finish with the traditional formalities of karate.

In 2001 there was a special guest from Japan who visited the Crystal Palace course. Mr Muneyasu Hoshino who is the director of the JKA, attended to give a special speech to the students on the course. He explained the success of the 10-year legal battle that had ensued over the split in the JKA. The split occurred after the untimely death of the JKA Chief Instructor Master Nakayama. There were basically two factions of the JKA both calling themselves the official JKA. The situation had to be resolved in the courts of Japan to decide which of the two factions were the official JKA. The court's decision went to "our" JKA, the "Nakahara Faction" and Mr Hoshino was delighted to pass this information on to all present. Sensei Enoeda was very pleased with this news. The problems over

be lifted, as it was so heavy, being filled with coins and jewellery. One evening when she was asleep a terrible fire began in the house. She called the fire brigade and ran out of the house. Then she realised she had left all of her money and jewellery in the big suitcase underneath her bed. She didn't want to leave it behind and lose it in the fire. She ran back into the house and gathering all of her strength lifted the suitcase and carried it outside. After the case had been taken outside, it was discovered that nobody else could lift or even move the suitcase. Everyone wondered how this little old lady managed to get the suitcase out of the burning house. The answer is, when faced with adversity, you can achieve anything, even if it seems quite impossible."

Sensei Jim Wood entertains as McSochin

Japan were enthusiastically consumed by the audience. Film of JKA championships always went down well, as did some of the archive Enoeda TV adverts. Shortly after Sensei Enoeda arrived in the UK, he became involved in making some adverts for British TV. These adverts were captured on video and replayed at some of the parties, much to the amusement of all in attendance. One of the best adverts was for a popular brand of crisps, which featured Sensei Enoeda at the climax of the film punching through a bag of crisps accompanied by a blood curdling "kiai!". There were also adverts made for jeans, with Enoeda proving to the viewers that this particular brand of clothing was the hardest wearing that one could get! It was not uncommon to see film crews at the Marshall Street Dojo, filming an interview or perhaps a piece of documentary for a programme. Looking back on these films at the parties was

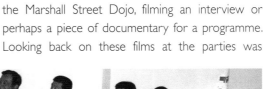

Sensei Ohta in fine voice

The late Sensei Tabata together with Tsuyama and Ohta always enjoyed the parties and dancing

extremely entertaining for everyone present.

The Japanese instructors seemed to lose all their inhibitions at these parties and greatly enjoyed singing for their audience. Backing tracks for this singing were often provided and a tape machine for this purpose was never far away. Most of the time the instructors would sing in Japanese but it made no difference; the audience loved every minute of it.

The last Crystal Palace course with Sensei Enoeda was in August 2002. Everyone received a course certificate

Whatever time the party finished or however merry the participants became, the instructors were always up bright and early the following morning. There was always an early 7.00am training session the next day, which took place before the regular Crystal Palace morning class. If the weather was fine, Sensei Enoeda would take some of the most dedicated students for a run and some special breathing exercises. Sensei Ohta would take the lead and Sensei Enoeda would be running alongside whilst chatting to any of the other runners nearby. Sensei Tabata, Osaka or Ohta would take an early morning kihon or kata class, sometimes revising the basic Shotokan kata. As many as thirty or as few as three would take these special early morning classes, when the dancing and the singing of the previous evening would be pushed to one side and karate would take pride of place once again.

Sensei Enoeda assists the "magician" with a wood breaking exercise that became a watch breaking exercise

were resident on the course enjoyed these parties immensely and always joined in with the fun and games. It seemed as though they wanted to escape the daily constraints of discipline within the dojo with their dancing, singing and fun-making. I do have one scene etched into my memory of Sensei Tanaka with a smoking cigarette stuffed up each nostril, doing his impersonation of a Japanese dragon breathing fire!

Everyone, including Sensei Enoeda, joined in with the dancing and the fun. There would be singing too and in true Japanese tradition, most of the resident Japanese instructors would at some point take the microphone and give good renditions of their favourite songs.

Sensei Jim Wood, the Chief Instructor of JKA Scotland, was also a great devotee of the parties and on one occasion entertained the crowd as "Mr Mc. Sochin", bent over a walking stick and dressed in a brightly coloured tartan karate gi! There would be "mock" sumo matches and "mock" golf tuition. All the different representative countries would join in and offer their own special brand of humour. The Japanese instructors who

The Crystal Palace parties were happy times; moments to let off steam and relax. Sensei Enoeda always seemed happy and proud whilst enjoying these fun times. The Crystal Palace parties sometimes got almost totally out of hand. Tricks were played endlessly on the poor long-suffering Japanese instructors. It was our light hearted way of getting our own back on the instructors for our aching bones and sore feet. Sensei Enoeda got to understand well the English sense of humour, but sometimes the jokes did get a little over the top and scary.

The three photos on this page show just how far Sensei Enoeda went along with the jokes that were played upon him. Eric Pich and Sue Sinclair invited Sensei Enoeda to

All is well that ends well. After the joke, the watch is returned; Eric and Sue are forgiven

Sensei Tabata and Sensei Osaka witness the strange British sense of humour

watch some Tameshewara (wood breaking) which was the start of the joke. Wood was offered to be broken with a karate strike. The action then carried the joke forward to the point where Sensei's expensive watch was being borrowed to assist with the trick. The "Tameshawara" then contiued with the watch being smashed to pieces with a large mallet in front of his very eyes! This was the point where the joke almost ended for Sensei Enoeda, however, what he did not realise is that his own very expensive watch had been secretly replaced with another cheap replica of the very same watch. The tension rose as the watch was smashed to pieces, and the incredulous look on Sensei Enoeda's face had to be seen to be believed. Later, after the joke had been explained, Sensei Enoeda actually picked up the broken pieces of watch from the floor, saying "Just in case". He was eventually presented with his own original watch

once again and thankfully there were smiles and laughter all round. One dreads to think what would have happened if the two watches were muddled up and the wrong watch was broken into tiny pieces.

Here is another joke that pushed the guest instructor's understanding of the British sense of humour to unimaginable heights: a play on words that must have been extremely difficult for any non-British person to understand.

The joke started innocently enough with a call for a Japanese kata. From that point, the action moved on to a "Thai kata". The words were then intentionally misrepresented and distorted to become "tie cutter". The complexities of the language at this point must have been almost impossible for Sensei Tabata and Osaka to understand, but nevertheless they went along bravely with the exercise.

I should explain that the guest instructors had previously been presented with a special ceremonial tartan tie from the Scottish representatives. They were then instructed that these ties should be worn straightaway so as not to cause offence.

When the guest instructors – Sensei Osaka and Sensei Tabata – requested to see the "Thai kata" (tie cutter), their ceremonial Scottish ties which were being worn, were sliced in half with a pair of scissors, to the delight of all present – except the instructors.

The list of gags, jokes and banter is endless, but it is certainly true to say that everyone who attended the Crystal Palace Courses and parties had a great time. The karate was brilliant, and the parties great fun.

The finish of another successful Crystal Palace course. Sensei Enoeda dancing with Gere Larson, Jim Wood, Peter Welsh, Eric Pich and Noel Casey

K1 JKA

SENSEI ENOEDA'S RELATIONSHIP WITH SCOTLAND grew and blossomed for more than thirty years. The people and flavours of the country were enticing, and at various times he found himself dressed in a kilt, travelling in a Rolls Royce and even as a guest of the Queen.

Far left: Jim Wood MBE with Sensei Enoeda at Buckingham Palace

Left: Jim Wood receives his MBE from the Queen

Sensei Enoeda's GS300 Lexus Saloon – K1 JKA

Jim Wood MBE was the JKA lynchpin for Sensei Enoeda's regular visits four or five times per year to Scotland. The relationship lasted for more than thirty years. Sensei Enoeda loved Scotland and described it as "the most beautiful country in the world".

The opening of Jim Wood's new dojo in Scotland by Sensei Enoeda, Tabata and Tsuyama

He also considered Scotland to be a particularly healthy place to live in and to visit. His family often accompanied him on these eagerly anticipated visits. He enjoyed Scotland in the autumn, with the golden tones and striking colours of the trees. The wonderful views in Scotland must have reminded him so much of his early years in Japan when the autumn colours of the trees, particularly the acers, are so very beautiful.

Although Sensei Enoeda was a Master in the dojo with the charisma of a Japanese warrior, I often saw him quite humbled by the wonders of nature. A starlit sky, a wonderful sunset, or even the scent of a newly mown grass field would have a very fundamental and moving effect on him. Certainly during the summer months when he visited our main dojo in Chingford, he would often stand by the wide open dojo doors and breathe in deeply the air and the scent of the large green sports field opposite. This was a side of him that few people saw, but I noticed that he always took the time to enjoy his natural surroundings wherever he was in the world. I believe he gained great enjoyment from these, the simple things in life and when in Scotland, he saw and enjoyed nature at its best.

Jim and the Scottish JKA members welcomed Sensei Enoeda as an old friend just as much as the chief instructor of JKA Europe. These visits took place for more than twenty-five years, sometimes four or five times per year. Sensei Enoeda often took along with him some of the top Japanese instructors to visit and teach in his beloved Scotland. Masters Tabata, Yahara, Osaka, Tanaka, Ueki, Tsuyama, and Mori plus many others all had a taste of Scotland, Scottish hospitality and karate. Jim always made sure that the organisation and planning for these visits were perfect, but the timetable had to include some golf at St Andrews, Gleneagles, Turnberry or Dornoch, together with some fun!

One of the highlights of the relationship that Jim had with Sensei Enoeda was in 1991 when Jim opened his own purpose-built karate dojo. Sensei Enoeda together with Sensei Tabata and Tsuyama travelled to Scotland for the event and performed an opening ceremony together with a special karate course, to get the new dojo successfully up and running.

The dojo, which Sensei Wood designed and built himself, is unique in Scotland and is indeed one of the very few purpose-built dojos in the United Kingdom. The dojo has the unique and prestigious honour of being twinned with the famous Takushoku University Karate Club in Japan. Takushoku was of course the university of Sensei Enoeda

A relaxing game of golf with some of the world's most senior karate instructors

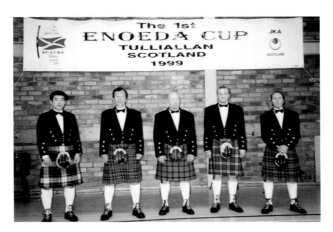

The senior JKA instructors wearing traditional Scottish attire.
Sensei Ohta, Enoeda, Bura, Larson and Wood

and Sensei Ohta. A specially designed plaque hangs in the dojo, which was presented on the opening day as a gift from the world-famous Professor of Karate-Do, Master Tsuyama of the Takushoku University in Tokyo.

In 1995 Sensei Enoeda gave his permission for Aileen Simpson 4th Dan, Jim's partner, to set up the "Tiger Cubs" section in the Scottish honbu. The Tiger Cubs were children between the ages of four and six who wished to learn Shotokan Karate within a specially designed junior format. This format provided a safer environment and a less disciplined atmosphere for the children, who would learn some Japanese words and phrases together with the basic skills of karate. There was to be no fighting or contact at this stage, but the children would earn tags as their abilities improved. The accumulation of these tags would eventually lead to a child attempting a full grading for 9th Kyu. Mrs Enoeda was also involved in the planning of this project and helped by choosing a name for the Tiger Cubs logo. After much discussion, the name ASUNARO was arrived at. Mrs Enoeda explained that in Japan there

Jim cuts a celebration cake with Mr Hoshino

are two trees, the Asunaro and the Hinoki, one being a smaller variety of the larger tree. The combination of the words ASU and NARO mean growing tomorrow. Mrs Enoeda felt that the name Asunaro was most suitable for the Tiger Cubs, as they would hopefully aspire to being as strong and fearless as the fully grown Enoeda tiger. The extremely successful Tiger Cubs format has now been introduced to other dojos in Scotland as well as the JKA operation in Australia organised by Jim and Aileen.

The first JKA Scotland Masters Camp was held in 1999 and hosted Sensei Enoeda, Ohta, and Bura the JKA Chief instructor of Holland, together with Gere Larson, the JKA Chief instructor of Norway. Jim made the instructor's historic visit to Scotland most memorable with the traditional Scottish kilt and sporran being worn by all the instructors for a group photograph.

Sensei Enoeda shares a drink with JKA director Mr Hoshino

In 2001 there was a "Legends" course with Masters Mori from the USA, and Ueki and Hoshino from Japan. Master Mori is a legend in his own right and Mr Muneyasu Hoshino is the director of the JKA Santama Branch.

Jim is, and always has been, a staunch supporter of the JKA, and it was his idea to make a special gift to Sensei Enoeda, involving his new Lexus car. The gift took the shape of a special personalised number plate – K1 JKA. The "K" of course standing for Keinosuke. Sensei's wife Reiko, as an intimate and personal name for her husband, always used the nickname "K" (Kei). This was always a source of fun between Sensei Enoeda and his wife Reiko, who often joked that "K" (Kay) was a girl's name, and the shortened version of Reiko, Rei (Ray), was a

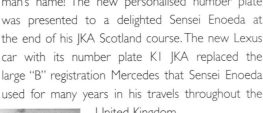

The JKA Scotland purpose built dojo

man's name! The new personalised number plate was presented to a delighted Sensei Enoeda at the end of his JKA Scotland course. The new Lexus car with its number plate K1 JKA replaced the large "B" registration Mercedes that Sensei Enoeda used for many years in his travels throughout the United Kingdom.

There were indeed many great experiences that Sensei Enoeda gained from his connection with Scotland. He was pictured in a kilt at one of Jim Wood's Scottish Masters Camp parties, although it is debatable whether or not this was a truly enjoyable experience for him. He was dressed in top hat and tails (formal attire) at Buckingham Palace when Jim received his MBE from the Queen, for services to karate in 1999. The pair even ven-

At St Andrews in Scotland. Sensei Wood, Enoeda, Hoshino and Mori together with, on the far right, Dr Bill Carr and his son, who originated Transports of Delight

tured into sumo wrestling at one of the Crystal Palace parties, with £5 on the floor for the winner! Jim attended 47 of the Crystal Palace courses over the years and had a personal ambition to reach 50.

There was another bonus for Sensei Enoeda and the various JKA instructors when visiting Scotland. Doctor Bill Carr, an aptly named collector of rare quality automobiles and motorcycles, on occasion used one of his prized Rolls Royce "Silver Shadow" saloons as a special treat to collect and deliver the visiting instructors to various locations during their stay in Scotland. This gave the instructors a wonderful taste of luxury that was quite rare.

Doctor Bill Carr, who has attained the rank of Black Belt, started karate in 1969 and has been a student of Jim Wood for more than twenty years. Bill is the proprietor of a company called Transports of Delight, set up in 1994 to capitalise on his collection of unique cars and motorcycles. The company, now well established, offers a luxury car service for weddings and other special occasions. It so happened that when in Scotland, Sensei Enoeda and the other Japanese instructors were often taken to and from the airport in a Rolls Royce "Silver Shadow" and even taken to and from the golf club at St Andrews in the same vehicle. Sensei Enoeda got on very well with Bill and was always intrigued and entertained when travelling in one of Bill's beautiful vehicles.

There was unfortunately no such luxury

in London for Sensei Enoeda. I would sometimes collect him from his home and deliver him back safely after he had completed one of our London gradings or a "Masterclass". After the event we would have a meal and a few drinks. Sensei Enoeda would then be crammed into my small Toyota MR2 and sleep the journey away noisily, with his shoes off – feet up on the dashboard. This kind of journey did not compare at all favourably with the luxury transport facilities that he received in Scotland. However, he never complained; sleep was probably a way of escaping the lack of comfort in the journey.

Bill's whole family is involved in the car business. One of his sons is a racing driver and another is a student of car design, Bill, as well as running Transports of Delight, is also a general practitioner and has for many years been present at the JKA Scotland championships in his capacity as a doctor.

When Jim and Aileen moved to Australia in 2002, Sensei Enoeda gave some very specific advice to Jim. "Do not change anything in your karate; keep following the way of Enoeda – the way of the JKA." Jim had no intention of doing otherwise, but nevertheless the advice has been and will always be, well remembered, etched into the mind and acted upon by Jim, Aileen and all the members of JKA Scotland.

A sumo match with £5 on the floor for the winner!

Golf

THE CRACK OF THE GOLF BALL or the snap of the karate gi. Both of these sounds were more than familiar to Sensei Enoeda. When karate finished there was golf – another challenge and a way to relax and socialise. The two activities brought him great pleasure and a sense of personal achievement.

Sensei Enoeda enjoying a joke on the green

Is there a link between golf and karate? It is hard to imagine two activities that are so different – or are they? Certainly, many who practice karate also gain great satisfaction from playing golf and indeed some excel in both of these activities. The hips may have a similar swing. The focus and concentration required to deliver the ball to its required destination may be similar to that required to make a good punch reach its target. I do know that golf players, like karate enthusiasts, get totally hooked on the game and talk, eat, drink and think golf.

Sensei Enoeda loved his game of golf; he also loved watching it on TV. I remember when a few of us from Marshall Street were helping to move Sensei Enoeda and his family to his new home in Kingston. His main concern was to find the Sky Sports channel on his TV and tune in to the golf championship highlights being shown. Chairs, tables, bookcases and boxes were being hoisted through windows and hauled upstairs, however Sensei Enoeda was oblivious to all the noise and chaos surrounding him and sat on the bare floor a few inches away from the television. He was cheering on the golf players whilst we were all grunting, groaning and sweating moving all the furniture into the new home. It was a bizarre

sight and we all had a good laugh about it over a cup of tea later in the day.

It is fair to say that the bulk of Sensei Enoeda's spare time was spent playing and enjoying golf. Certainly when the weather was fine he could often be found at his own club, Coombe Hill, or at Wentworth. This is not to say that the weather was the catalyst that decided if golf was to be played or not. Far from it! "In England if you rely on the weather for a game of golf you will NEVER play," was how he admonished his long time golf partner Mariko Watanabe, when she enquired if a planned game of golf was going ahead in the pouring rain. Needless to say, the game went ahead.

To some extent when karate finished, golf took over. It would be unusual if Sensei Enoeda didn't check out the golfing facilities that were available near the

karate course venues that he visited. St Andrews and Gleneagles in Scotland were obvious choices to mix some great karate with some excellent golf in wonderful surroundings.

Although the karate courses were always packed, there were generally some instructors and students who would share Sensei Enoeda's love of golf and steer him towards the local golf course after the karate training had finished.

Jim Wood MBE, the Chief instructor for JKA Scotland, always ensured that when in Scotland, time would be found for a game or two of golf at Dornoch, Turnberry, St Andrews or Gleneagles. Most of the JKA instructors that Sensei Enoeda brought over to the United Kingdom enjoyed their game of golf, particularly in Scotland where there are so many wonderful courses.

Nearer to home, Sensei Enoeda played golf regularly with his wife Reiko and long-time karate students Craig Raye and Mariko Watanabe. There would also be happy times spent together on the golf course with his friend Mr Shu and ladies champion Keiko Yamada Pou and even at times Jimmy Tarbuck. He and his wife Reiko were both members of their local golf club, Coombe Hill, and played regularly together on the course. Reiko remembers being introduced to golf by her husband when she was just 25 years old. "It was freezing cold and snowing and at that time I really did not want to play golf. I did however continue and started to really enjoy the game, now I try to play regularly and improve."

Mariko Watanabe won the Tiger Cup Ladies

The Enoeda swing

Championship in 2002 with a net score of 139. She kindly offered to take me to Wentworth golf course to meet Sensei Enoeda's long time golf caddy and good friend Kevin Jarman. I learnt more about golf that day than I ever knew before! Kevin explained to me the subtle and supportive relationship that exists between a golf player and a caddy. Complete knowledge of every inch of the course together with distance, wind direction and velocity plus general weather conditions are the ambits of a good caddy. Often little is said or proffered but advice is subtly given as to which golf club or iron should be used. This advice was often completely ignored by Sensei Enoeda and when a five iron was suggested his favourite Yonex four iron was insisted upon! When the ball overshot its target by a considerable distance, guess who got the blame?

Sensei Enoeda regularly played at Wentworth usually with Kevin as his caddy. It was obvious to me that Kevin had a great relationship during his eight years caddying for Sensei Enoeda. He enjoyed his company as well as the golf.

I had to ask Kevin the ultimate question, "Was he good?" Kevin deftly sidestepped and respectfully countered with some wonderful compliments and anecdotes about his time with "K" as he was affectionately known.

"He never got angry, but took everything in his stride. He did hit a few good birdies and was playing at his best two to three years previously (2000–2001). Lunch or a few pounds would often be wagered on a game. He did beat me once, but refused to take

A golfing holiday in Ireland. Mr and Mrs Enoeda with Mrs Tomita

the money we had wagered. 'K' would arrive early in the morning, hours before the others that he would be playing, to practise and to improve his handicap of thirteen. He would have breakfast and then practice on the golf range or the putting green. We would start the game and he would soon be talking about what was for lunch!"

On one occasion Wentworth was completely closed due to very wet weather. The scheduled game with Mr Shu and Kevin was unable to be played. However "K" was determined and telephoned all of the local golf clubs to see if any were open. He finally drove the golfing party in his own car, miles away, to the Buckinghamshire club, which was open, insisting on playing the game.

There was also a funny side to some of the golf stories and at this particular event a while later, some students got their own revenge on Sensei Enoeda. It was at one of the Crystal Palace parties that were held in the evening after the training and grading. A "golf instructor" was on hand at the party, to give Sensei Enoeda a golf lesson in order to improve his

Golfing partner Mariko Watanabe with Kevin Jarman, Sensei Enoeda's caddy

technique. Each time he took a swing at the imaginary ball with his club, the swing was dismissed as "No good – try again". This happened a few times and then it was suggested that a real golf ball should now be used. The doors of the party room opened out on to the fields of the Crystal Palace grounds. A "golf ball" was put in place at the open doorway and the instructions were to strike the ball hard and send it out onto the field. Sensei Enoeda took an enormous swing at the ball and didn't miss. There was an almighty explosion. It was an exploding golf ball! The whole room erupted in laughter especially at the look of shock on Sensei Enoeda's face.

Jim Kelly, one of the original Marshall Street members, took Sensei Enoeda to one of the Bob Hope Classics, a glittering celebrity filled golf tournament, which was held at the Moor Park golf course at Rickmansworth in the south of England. Sensei Enoeda enjoyed this day greatly, mixing with all of the famous celebrities and some of the world's top golfers. For once he was not the centre of attention or the star of the show and he liked it. Jim recalled a conversation on that day about a possible relationship between a golf handicap and a dan grade standard. Sensei Enoeda related it thus. A three handicap = 1st Dan. Scratch or no handicap = 3rd Dan. Below scratch = 4th or 5th Dan. Only someone who is good at golf and also good at karate will know if there is fact in this theory, but it is an interesting thought. If we

Mr Kevin Jarman, Sensei Enoeda's golf caddy at Wentworth

carry this thought further forward and perform a little crafty calculation, we can see that this theory does not in fact work to Sensei Enoeda's advantage. With a handicap of thirteen, he would actually become a green or purple belt in the golfing world – if we interpreted the results of these calculations literally!

Sensei Enoeda really got interested in golf during the 1960s whilst taking part in the JKA world tour and his travels abroad. Sensei Stan Schmidt, the JKA Chief instructor in South Africa, recalls those early days of golf with Enoeda. "I resigned from my job, and had my mornings free. Our afternoons and evenings were devoted to teaching beginners and advanced students. After Enoeda and I had finished our early morning training, the rest of our mornings became occupied with two main things: swimming at a nearby pleasure resort and learning to play golf. Sam Belnick,

The Crystal Palace parties included golf – this time with an exploding golf ball!

a lawyer black belt who had a farm in Rustenburg (a ninety-minute drive from Johannesburg), invited us to play golf at the Rustenburg course with a top businessman. Up until this point we had played actual golf about three times and this was our first actual golf invitation match. We were real rookies at the game. Enoeda and I used an old number three wood and a seven iron when we visited a nearby driving range."

"We had better buy some decent clubs," I suggested. "Of course," he beamed. So we visited the Pro Golf Shop. I didn't have much money in those days, nor did Enoeda, so I scratched around and came up with about 25 or 30 Rand. With this we naively set out to buy two sets of clubs. After spending an entire morning at the golf shop trying and testing the most superb clubs, we walked out of there with three second-hand clubs, six balls, and a packet of tees. Under Enoeda's arm was a box containing a pair of neat, spiked golf shoes, and on his head he wore a new golf cap. We were ready for Rustenburg. We hopped into my old Volvo and were on our way."

"We kept promising each other how we were going to annihilate the two Rustenburg golfers. Sam Belnick, Enoeda and I spent a relaxed and enjoyable evening sitting outside Sam's big farmhouse, which was on an orange farm on the Golden Mile near Rustenburg. We were watching a magnificent sunset, sipping beer and grilling different types of meat on the log fire. The main talk was how we were going to whip Sam and his partner at the following day at golf."

"At 6:00 o'clock, I awoke. The first thing I saw through by window was what looked like Ben Hogan himself. A second glance told me that it was Enoeda, complete with golf cap and golf shoes, warming up,

Stuck in a bunker at St Andrews in Scotland

Senei Enoeda and Sensei Ueki enjoying the golf and the fresh air

hitting at an imaginary ball. He really looked the part. "Ohayo, gozai masu, Sensei," I shouted through the open window. "Osu Stan, today I feel very good", he shouted. "You look good Sensei, I hope we both break 100 today." "Of course!" he shouted, sending an imaginary ball into the distant Blue Mountains."

"As we arrived at the members' entrance in Sam's Mercedes Benz, our golf opponent stood waiting. He was perfectly attired in spiked shoes, smart slacks, golf cap, and leather gloves, and a huge state-of-the-art golf bag and kit stood regally between him and his caddie. "This man is very serious about his golf," said Sam. "Is that so?" I replied. Inside, I was saying "Oh, no!" I glanced at Enoeda. He merely winked one of his cat's eyes at me, as if saying, "Not worry, Stan.'"

"As we stepped out of Sam's car, a horde of motley-clad, adolescent caddies descended upon us. We chose three and dismissed the rest, who stood there watching. Sam opened the boot of his car and handed his bag to the first caddie. The other two caddies were waiting to shoulder our two

bags, which of course, were non-existent. Instead, I handed two clubs to one caddie and three clubs to the other. Then I handed each of them a sock with three golf balls in it and a few tees. The two caddies had never seen this sort of thing before, and they couldn't hide their surprise. Their mouths were wide open as we handed them our pitiful equipment. This was not lost on Enoeda. The look on his face had me clutching my sides trying to suppress my mirth, but now was not the time. I told the caddies to move on to the first tee quickly. I didn't want to shake up our Mr Vermeulen too much. Sam introduced us as two champions from Japan. Through habit, Enoeda and I bowed to Mr Vermeulen. Both of us said "Osu!" Not much more was said as Sam and Mr.

Some of the world's top karate instructors played golf at St Andrews in Scotland

A good swing!

ermeulen became engaged in some discussion as we approached the first tee."

"After we had duffed our first drives, I overheard Mr Vermeulen talking to Sam in Afrikaans, "But I thought you said they were Japanese champions?" It hadn't taken long for Vermeulen to discover that Enoeda and I were not golf pros from Japan. "No, Vermeulen," laughed Sam, "don't be stupid. They're karate champions." I noticed that Vermeulen maintained a respectable distance from us for the rest of the game. Enoeda and I chatted with each other in a mixture of broken English and Japanese that only the two of us could understand. For instance, when I hit a fresh-air shot, Enoeda remarked "More kime (focus) Stan," and I responded with "Osu, Sensei!""

"Sam drifted between Vermeulen and the pair of us, always the considerate gentlemen conveying messages of praise at even the lamest of shots. One time Enoeda uttered a loud "kiai" as he teed off. A golfer in another foursome nearby, who was attempting a

Sensei Mori, Enoeda and Ueki together with JKA Director Mr Hoshino

close putt at the time missed the hole. Vermeulen, who knew the group, just gave a sheepish smile and averted his gaze towards the distant mountains."

"One time, near the end of our very hot and laborious game, it took me about four attempts to get the confounded ball out of a bunker. I overheard Vermeulen whisper in the Afrikaans language to Sam, "That tall Jap with the sunglasses isn't as good as the other one." Sam dropped his putter and doubled up. "Vermeulen, you nit-wit. The tall guy might walk like a Japanese and talk like a Japanese, but he's no Japanese." "What!" Vermeulen moved closer to Sam. "Now I've really messed things up," he whispered. "Who the hell is he, then?" "That's Stan Schmidt. He's a South African who has just trained in Japan. He's not Japanese!" Later, in the pub, Sam explained to Enoeda Sensei what had happened. Enoeda was so tickled by this episode that he exploded with laughter, slapping the table. The drinks and peanuts flew in all directions. "Very funny!" he shouted and kept repeating, "Mistaah Stan, like man from Japan! Ha, ha, ha!" Enoeda's laughter was infectious. Soon every person in the pub was laughing along with him.

The Books and Videos

H OW FORTUNATE WE ARE to have karate textbooks available by Masters Gichin Funakoshi, Masatoshi Nakayama and countless others. The information and pictures passed down to us over the years serve as a great database of information, knowledge and history. When I visited the Hoitsukan in Tokyo – Nakayama Sensei's dojo – the series of *Best Karate* handbooks he had written were on display, taking pride of place close to the Shomen, or dojo front. Thankfully it seems almost obligatory for karate masters to put pen to paper and inspire us. Sensei Enoeda produced some excellent videotapes as well as karate handbooks.

KARATE –
DEFENCE and ATTACK

The first book that Sensei Enoeda produced is in fact a gem. Published in 1972, just a few years after he settled in England, this small book is entitled *Karate – Defence and Attack*. Although the quality of printing is not very good, the photography in the little book is superb. Frank Elliot was a cinematographer, and his pictures show Enoeda dressed smartly in fashionable tight trousers, jacket and tie, performing all manner of karate techniques in full view of the popular tourist landmarks and attractions in the City of London. The Royal Horseguards, the Tower of London, Tower Bridge, Big Ben and Trafalgar Square all act as dramatic backdrops for Enoeda, defending against knife, gun and chair attacks. The tourists present at these locations must have been very surprised at what they saw being photographed and were probably quite worried too. Some very

effective self defence is included, using knee, elbow, foot and hand techniques.

The book is unique in that it shows Enoeda performing some incredible karate fully dressed in conventional clothing, the trousers of which appear quite tight fitting. The kicks and punches however do look absolutely stunning. There is even a sequence of pictures that show Enoeda defending against an attack whilst he is sitting in his Ford Capri! Fabulous stuff!

It is not the regular type of karate book or manual, but is worth looking out for just for the pictures alone. Sensei Enoeda was assisted by Sensei Kato together with John Chisholm and the book was published by Paul H. Crompton.

SHOTOKAN KARATE –
FREE FIGHTING TECHNIQUES

Shotokan Karate – Free Fighting Techniques was also published in the 1970s, again by Paul H. Crompton. This must have been one of the very first books published that deals purely with kumite techniques and although only 85 pages in length,

it is packed with photos, descriptions and useful Japanese terminology. The book is a manual of ippon kumite defences and attacks which progress from Kihon Ippon kumite to Jiyu Ippon kumite and ultimately Jiyu kumite. Sensei Tomita together

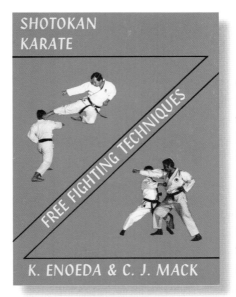

with Mr Charles Mack are used throughout the book as the attackers. Sensei Tomita acted as an assistant to Sensei Enoeda for ten years, and Charles Mack is credited with being a 3rd Dan karate black belt as well as holding 5th Dan in judo and 1st Dan in Aikido.

The book shows Enoeda performing his famous Ashi Barai (leg sweep) together with basic and advanced kumite defences and attacks. Shortly after this book was published, Master Nakayama wrote in his *Best Karate Volume 4*, "Keinosuke Enoeda has a reputation for achievements that stir the imagination. Using the power of thoroughly strengthened legs and loins, he delivers strikes and kicks of great force, which cannot be blocked easily with simple

evasive tactics. His ashi barai (leg sweep), which uses the whole body, is very strong. Especially amazing is his ability to cut in deeply, catch his opponent's supporting leg and send him flying. As shown by his past record, Enoeda has mastered these tactics and many an opponent has tasted the cup of defeat. He could not have reached this level without abundant fundamental training of legs and hips day by day."

Both *Shotokan Karate – Free Fighting Techniques'* and *Best Karate Volume 4* show some great pictures of Enoeda demonstrating these various ashi barai techniques to gain total domination over his opponents.

SHOTOKAN KARATE

Released in 1978, this rare film was made available by EMI and shown on London Weekend Television at the time of release.

The format was full colour on a Super 8 film cassette. The film is very advanced for the time it was made, as it shows kihon, kata and kumite filmed in quality slow motion as well as normal speed.

Sensei Tomita is the sparring partner for Sensei Enoeda during the kumite section of this film and the action finishes with a great flying side kick and "kiai" by Enoeda in brilliant slow motion.

If you can get hold of a copy you will need an old Super 8 film projector to show it. It may however be available on video from one or two suppliers.

SHOTOKAN – ADVANCED KATA

The set of three *Advanced Kata* volumes are most sought after as reference manuals for the Shotokan kata, and are difficult to get hold of as they are often out of print. Dragon Books first published this set of three books in 1983 and there have been subsequent reprints. The fourth or final book of this series covering the Kata Meikyo, Unsu and, interestingly, two versions of Wankan was never published. A few years ago I asked Sensei Enoeda when and if this final volume was going to be published. "Bruddy Pubrishers", he brusquely answered. That sort of answered my question and it didn't seem as though any further explanation would be forthcoming. Nevertheless, it is a shame that the

fourth and last Enoeda kata book never appeared to complete the series of Kata books.

I understand that the latest publishers of the books, Sakura, moved their business to the USA and were unable to allow further publication of the books in England.

Mrs Chieko Buck added some attractive Japanese calligraphy to this set of books. She also made translations of the meaning of the various kata, giving depth to the names of kata such as Gankaku and Gojushiho.

The photography for

the books was completed in London with Sensei Enoeda assisted by Sensei Tomita and Terry O'Neill. Sensei Tomita recalls that the photography did not go at all smoothly and Sensei Enoeda after seeing the "rush" contact prints often insisted on redoing photographic sequences. Nevertheless, the final

BEGINNER TO BLACK BELT: THE MASTER TEXT

Produced by the "Tiger Corporation" in 1994, this comprehensive videotape covers all of the basic combinations, kata and kumite from the level of novice white belt up to the level required for black belt. Allan Barrett, a professional cameraman and lighting technician, who is also a Shotokan black belt, did the filming for this first-class video. The video opens with some pure Shotokan techniques performed by Enoeda. He also demonstrates beautifully some of his favourite kata applications. Sensei Ohta and Jim Lewis assist throughout.

Kihon Kata, the five Heian Kata, Tekki Shodan and Bassai Dai are all filmed in great detail.

Three Step Sparring (Sanbon Kumite), One Step Sparring (Ippon Kumite) and Semi-Free Sparring are all demonstrated superbly. There is also the added bonus of Sensei Enoeda's special demonstration of kata and kumite, which includes his infamous defence against four opponents. The kata devised by Enoeda himself, is temporally interrupted in mid flow, by four attackers. The four are dispensed with promptly and the kata is subsequently resumed and completed in Sensei Enoeda's own inimitable way. This video is perfect in that it shows close up and in full graphic detail the famous display that Enoeda devised and which was used

results are excellent and the books stand up well after 20 years, as a useful tool for improving or revising one's kata knowledge.

for many years at the KUGB National Championships.

In all there are nine sections to this video, which runs for just over one hour. I believe Sensei Enoeda was very pleased with the finished results of this production. He did actually sit at his desk for some considerable time carefully signing one hundred of the boxes for the finished video. You may find that you have one of these special limited edition videos. The unique signature is written in gold ink on the front of the box.

SHOTOKAN KARATE
VOLUME 1: 10TH KYU TO 5TH KYU
VOLUME 2: 5TH KYU TO BLACK BELT

This two-volume set of books really goes hand in hand with the video *Beginner to Black Belt*. The two books show all of the combinations, kata and kumite that are required for a student's progress, from beginner and up to Black Belt 1st Dan.

Assisted by Sensei Y. Ohta and long-standing member of the Marshall Street SKC, Jim Lewis, the 350 pictures of all the kihon, kata and kumite are clear and very well photographed. There are also photographs of the key points in the application of kata which are, again, clear and easy to understand. Contained at the beginning of each book is also information on Master Gichin Funakoshi together with the history of Shotokan Karate and the background to the JKA. Some wonderful calligraphy is again used in both of these books, and this was created by Mrs Chieko Buck.

Published by AC Black in 1996, these books are well worth having for the novice to use as a guide through the various Kyu Grades up to Shodan and for the more advanced student as a reference manual.

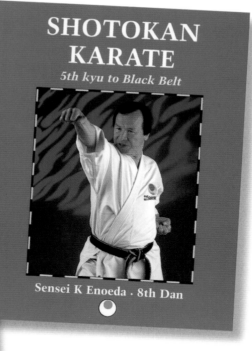

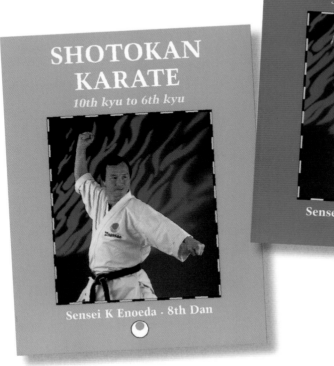

ADVANCED SHOTOKAN KATA (Volumes 1 to 4)

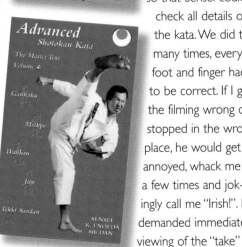

This series of four videos, which include twenty of the advanced black and brown belt katas, was filmed on Friday 26th October 1996 at Mentmore Towers, the stately home in Bedfordshire, England. The set of four kata videos were intended to follow on from the previously released *Beginner to Black Belt* video so that all of the Shotokan katas would be available in video format. The complete filming of all of the katas was completed in only one day starting at 8.00am and finishing at 8.00pm. The preparation however took much longer. I was volunteered to assist with this preparation, which ran for four weeks starting every morning at 7.00am. I would often be on my own with Sensei Enoeda for these rehearsals, filming every detail of each kata that he performed. I would always arrive at Marshall Street early to find Sensei Enoeda already in his gi and working on the makiwara (upright striking pad). He would always start the day like this and finish it in the same way. Usually around 200 Gyaku Zuki would be performed on each side, right and left during each of the morning

and afternoon makiwara sessions. We did the complete preparation, trial run through and test filming of the videos at the Marshall Street Dojo. The detail of every move and technique had to be perfect. I filmed with my old Super 8 video camera on a tripod, that I had used over the years for holidays. We then played the tape back on a TV monitor, so that Sensei could check all details of the kata. We did this many times, every foot and finger had to be correct. If I got the filming wrong or stopped in the wrong place, he would get annoyed, whack me a few times and jokingly call me "Irish!". He demanded immediate viewing of the "take" and gave me little time to rewind the tape to find the start of the action. Needless to say it was hard work and I had to learn to get faster and faster so that the shots could be seen and analysed almost straightaway. Sensei Ohta performed some of the katas in the rehearsals and at these times I would be doing the filming while Sensei Enoeda would be checking and analysing every move that was made by Sensei Ohta.

Books including the Nakayama *Best* series were checked for various differences in the katas, and reams of notes were made on the details that needed to be emphasised. International telephone calls to other senior JKA instructors were made, and I remember particular discrepancies were discussed for a long time regarding the Tate Zuki (upright punch) in the kata Chinte.

On the 24th October, two days before the actual filming was to take place, we made a final run through of the order for the video filming. At the same time, Sensei Enoeda checked which Karate gi to wear on the day of the shoot. He preferred the Tokaido fit, but this gi did not have a JKA badge in place. The Hirota gi had the JKA badge but wasn't such a good fit. He spent some time deliberating over this and asked me to take his car to a car park, as it was parked outside on a double yellow line (an immediate parking ticket offence in London's West End), while he decided which gi to take. I took the keys and with great difficulty drove his enormous automatic 'B' registration Mercedes around the narrow back streets of Soho. By my own admission I am not a good driver and I felt this was some sort of strange test I had been given. I was used to driving a small and noisy Toyota, and this Mercedes was so quiet I continually thought it had stalled and so I kept trying to restart the engine that was already running. Around one hour later after successfully parking the car, I returned to the Marshall Street Dojo and I found him on his makiwara with his gi jacket top off, rhythmically striking the pad. His hips were making a strong 45-degree twist and the striking was not particularly heavy but more like a solid and rhythmic thud. The unused hikite arm was hang-

Sensei Enoeda performs the kata Hangetsu

ing loosely at his side and the power seemed to be coming purely from the hips. He finally stopped and an incredulous Sensei Enoeda whacked me again for taking so long to park the car. These whacks were always very light hearted and I had the feeling that they were his own personal way of saying thanks or hello.

Sometimes during or after this preparation at Marshall Street we would go out for lunch or dinner. Usually we went to a Japanese restaurant or sushi bar nearby. These were very nice relaxed times when we would eat, joke and talk about the video tapes that were going to be made. I remember one conversation about Tekki Sandan where Sensei Enoeda explained that he had been practising the "old" version of the kata for more than twenty years, but now he had to get more used to the "new" version, as the JKA in Japan had seemingly dropped the old version. He made a mistake once whilst filming a rehearsal of Tekki Sandan and laughed out loud whilst mocking his own mistake. Certainly on occasion I have seen him teaching both versions of Tekki Sandan back to back with no difficulty whatsoever. However, most of us in that class would have great difficulty in performing these two katas and understanding the subtle differences in the two.

On another occasion he asked my opinion of a section of kata that we watched on the rehearsal tapes. He filmed two versions of Jitte and asked me what the difference was. I gave my idea of what I considered to be the main difference. "Nearly", he said, but he didn't tell me what the actual difference was!

Whilst rehearsing the application to Wankan, I was asked to assist with the application. Shoes off and in my jeans I felt strange but very honoured. Power, accuracy and kime were all very evident at this closest point to Sensei Enoeda.

Sensei Enoeda defends against a Bo attack in the kata Jitte

When later on it came to shooting the real video with a professional video team, in the film studio at Mentmore Towers, I went along, purely out of interest. We started out at 6.00am to arrive at Mentmore by 8.00am. Sensei Enoeda and Ohta stretched and loosened up while the equipment and lighting were being set up. Two professional cameramen were of course hired to do the filming, but there was a problem with one of the cameramen who arrived late. Sensei's voice boomed out – "Rod, YOU do it!". After explaining that I was not a REAL cameraman, I still had to do it, or be faced with the wrath of Sensei Enoeda. Of course I had never operated a large, fully professional camera on tracks like this in my life. I tried to appear reasonably confident and with a lot of help from the chief cameraman, Graham Reed, did my level best. The second poor cameraman was left redundant and eventually went home. I had very mixed feeling about taking over his job.

The filming was going slowly, too slowly for Sensei Enoeda. Sections of kata were filmed again and again; the tension and the heat was rising. The director said we would be unable to finish on schedule by the end of the day unless something was done. It was decided that three katas per hour together with the applications had to be filmed in order to keep to the schedule which had been planned. We all worked continuously, only stopping for a twenty-minute lunch break and again for short moments when more film had to be loaded into the cameras. Sensei Enoeda and Ohta had total concentration during these twelve hours of filming. The stamina and enthusiasm of both men never flagged at all during this time.

Close up on Enoeda

The filming of the videos was taken very seriously indeed and I could see that karate was almost like a religion to Sensei Enoeda. He was totally steeped in it and wanted perfection – quickly! He was impatient and couldn't stand fools, incompetence or someone who asked a stupid question. He watched and analysed his own kata sections that were filmed very closely and often said "once more", with everyone leaping to readiness in order to do another take. He was always very professional in front of the cameras and I assumed that this was because he had done some filming in the past for television advertising and chat shows. I felt mentally exhausted after four or five hours and was amazed at the mental stamina of both Sensei Enoeda and Ohta.

He seemed pleased when the filming was finally over and I found him outside waiting for everyone else to come out. Sensei Enoeda, usually impatient, did not like to hang around and wait for anyone. However on this occasion it was very dark outside. We were deep in the countryside, and there was no light pollution from roads or motorways. At this time he did not seem to mind waiting for the others but seemed relaxed and happy. He was quietly looking at the full moon and the bright stars in the sky and we both stood there for quite a time enjoying the perfect quietness and the beautiful clear October night sky illuminated by a million bright stars.

Enoeda and Ohta sit and watch a replay of the initial filming on video monitors

Get A Point!
The Lessons

THE COMMANDS "Get a point!", "Just one more!" or "Jodan!" were the short, sharp and effective words that drove us on and on to achieve more in our karate training. The words in themselves are simple enough, but it was Enoeda's voice, character and spirit that made them so effective and impossible to ignore.

Undoubtedly the most important gifts that Master Enoeda left his millions of karate followers all over the world were his lessons, the magic that we all felt being in his presence and being taught and trained by him. For this reason I have included in this section notes and pictures of some of his lessons, which I have tried to re-create with photographs and descriptions. This is probably like someone trying to describe a piece of music or a painting with words – an impossible task. However, over many years I did find a certain theme that ran through many of the classes and courses that I took with Sensei Enoeda. A pattern often emerged and I learnt to anticipate to some degree what was forthcoming in a class, by the first few moves of a set of techniques or a certain combination of moves. This is not to say the classes themselves were predictable. No one could ever say that! He always brought

something to a class that took you by surprise, or caught you unawares, taking you to new or higher ground – somewhere you had not visited before. Some of the following pictures describe combinations that were used in groups of two or three students as a kumite drill and some describe the practical applications to kata. These were some of my favourite lessons that I have collected over the years in note form. These descriptions of lessons are by no means comprehensive and by nature could never be called complete. That is not my intention. However, it may be in a small way, a means to recollect some of the really enjoyable and great moments in the classes that we shared with "The Boss," as he was affectionately called by some in England who were very close to him. The following lessons are just a few of my favourites, demonstrated here by Lucy Traettino, Gary James, Hachem Salem-Tedj and Stewart Grant.

Sanbon Kumite (Three Step Sparring) Using Kokutsu Dachi

1. Attacker steps forward three times with Oi Zuki Jodan starting from left Gedan Barai

2. Defender steps back three times blocking Age Uke in Kokutsu Dachi. The first block is with the right arm, the left leg steps back into left Kokutsu Dachi

3. The second is with the left arm blocking Age Uke, the right leg stepping back into right Kokutsu Dachi

4. The third is with the right arm blocking Age Uke, the left leg stepping back into left Kokutsu Dachi

5. The defender then counters with left Gyaku Zuki in Zenkutsu Dachi

Sanbon Kumite (Three Step Sparring) Using Kokutsu Dachi

1. Attacker steps forward three times with Oi Zuki Chudan starting from left Gedan Barai

2. Defender steps back three times blocking Uche Ude Uke in Kokutsu Dachi. The first block is with the right arm, the left leg stepping back into left Kokutsu Dachi

3. The second is with the left arm blocking Uche Ude Uke, the right leg stepping back into right Kokutsu Dachi

4. The third is with the right arm blocking Uche Ude Uke, the left leg stepping back into left Kokutsu Dachi

5. The defender then counters with left Gyaku Zuki in Zenkutsu Dachi

Sanbon Kumite (Three Step Sparring) Using Kokutsu Dachi

1. Attacker steps forward three times with Oi Zuki Chudan starting from left Gedan Barai

2. Defender steps back three times blocking Shuto Uke in Kokutsu Dachi. The first block is with the right hand, the left leg stepping back into left Kokutsu Dachi

3. The second is with the left hand blocking Shuto Uke, the right leg stepping back into right Kokutsu Dachi

4. The third is with the right hand blocking Shuto Uke, the left leg stepping back into left Kokutsu Dachi

5. The defender then counters with left Gyaku Zuki in Zenkutsu Dachi

Application for Heian Shodan (move numbers 1, 2, 3, and 4)

1. Attacker to the left of the defender steps forward with Oi Zuki Chudan

2. Defender from Yoi position, turns left and steps forward blocking Gedan Barai

3. The defender then steps forward with Oi Zuki Chudan; the attacker steps away

4. The second attacker from behind, steps forward with Oi Zuki Chudan. The defender turns and steps forward with Gedan Barai

5. The attacker then grabs the defender's wrist tightly

6. The defender twists his wrist anti-clockwise and pulls back to disengage the grip and unbalance the attacker

Heian Shodan continued......

7. **Finally pushing forward countering Jodan Tettsui Tate Mawashi Uche in Zenkutsu Dachi**

Defence Against Multiple Attack

1. **Attacker from left Gedan Barai steps forward with Oi Zuki Jodan plus three Chudan punches using only one step**

2. **Defender from Yoi position, steps back with left Age Uke**

3. **Then left Soto Ude Uke**

4. **Then left Gedan Barai**

Defence Against Multiple Attack continued......

5. **Then left Uche Ude Uke**

6. **Then counters with left Kizami Zuki Jodan**

7. **And right Gyaku Zuki, using only one step**

Application for Heian Yondan with two attackers and one defender
(move numbers 24, 25, 26 and 27)

1. **The first attacker steps forward from left Gedan Barai with right Oi Zuki Chudan**

2. **The defender steps back blocking left Chudan Morote Uke in right Kokutsu Dachi**

Heian Yondan continued.....

3. & 4. **The defender then grabs the attacker's head and counters with Hiza Geri, pushing the attacker away and turning to defend against the second attacker**

5 & 6. **The second attacker steps forward with Oi Zuki Chudan. The defender blocks this attack with left Shuto Uke in right Kokutsu Dachi, then brings the front foot back to adjust the distance**

7. **The defender then steps forward countering with right Jodan Shuto Uche**

8. **From this position the defender uses his front right leg to sweep the opponent with Ashi Barai**

Heian Yondan continued.....

9. **The right arm pushes forward and the right leg sweeps backward**

10. **The defender finishes with a left Gyaku Zuki**

Four Defences against Mae Geri (front kick)

1. **Both attacker and defender start from the Kamae position. The attacker steps forward with a right Mae Geri**

2. **Defender steps to the left, outside of attacker's kick and counters with left Kizami Zuki Jodan. The right arm is used to deflect the kick**

1. **Both attacker and defender start from the Kamae position. The attacker steps forward with a right Mae Geri**

2. **Defender steps forward and to the right and counters with right Oi Zuki Jodan. The left arm is used to deflect the kick**

Mae Geri continued.....

1. Both attacker and defender start from the Kamae position. The attacker steps forward with a right Mae Geri

2. Defender pushes to the right blocking with left Gedan Barai and countering with right Gyaku Zuki

1. Both attacker and defender start from the Kamae position. The attacker steps forward with a right Mae Geri

2. Defender pushes to the left blocking with left Nagashi Uke and countering with right Gyaku Zuki

Application for Heian Godan with two attackers and one defender
(move numbers 1, 2, 3, 4, 5, 6.)

1. & 2. The first attacker steps forward from left Gedan Barai with right Oi Zuki Chudan. The defender from the Yoi position steps left with left Uche Ude Uke in right Kokutsu Dachi

3. The defender then counters with right Chudan Gyaku Zuki in Kokutsu Dachi

4. The defender's punching arm then twists underneath the attacker's punching arm and pulls the attacker down. The right foot steps forward so that the feet are together

5. At this point the defender makes a left Kage Zuki to the back of the attackers head

6. The second attacker then steps forward with a left Oi Zuki Chudan. The defender makes a right Uche Ude Uke in left Kokutsu Dachi and a left Gyaku Zuki in Kokutsu Dachi

Heian Godan continued.....

7. **And then a left Gyaku Zuki in Kokutsu Dachi**

8. **The defender's punching arm then twists underneath the attacker's punching arm and pulls the attacker down**

9. **The left foot steps forward so that the feet are together. At this point the defender makes a right Kage Zuki to the back of the attacker's head**

Everyone in attendance when Sensei Enoeda included his kata application had a big treat! Two or three students would be picked from the class to perform a demonstration of the kata application. They would be told what to do once and then had to perform correctly in front of the class. Then everybody had to do it; correctly, straightway!

Sanbon Kumite Using Mawashi Geri

1. The attacker starts in left Zenkutsu Dachi, the defender in Yoi position. The attacker steps forward with a right Jodan Mawashi Geri

2. Defender steps back into right Zenkutsu Dachi blocking right Jodan Nagashi Uke

3. Defender then lifts knee

4. To counter with right Kizami Mawashi Geri

5. The attacker steps forward with a left Jodan Mawashi Geri. Defender steps back blocking left Jodan Nagashi Uke

5. He then lifts knee ready

Sanbon Kumite continued.....

6. **And counters with left Jodan Mawashi Geri**

7. **The attacker steps forward with the third Jodan Mawashi Geri. The defender steps back blocking right Jodan Nagashi Uke**

8. **The defender lifts the right knee**

9. **And counters with right Jodan Mawashi Geri**

Sensei Enoeda loved Mawashi Geri, Ura Mawashi Geri and Ushiro Mawashi Geri. We practised these kicks whilst lying down on the floor and also from a Zenkutsu Dachi position kicking off of the front leg. He always preferred students to target their kicks to JODAN in a kumite lesson and it was always very evident to see the enjoyment on his face when a student achieved this, using good timing, distance, control and accuracy.

Application for Bassai Dai with one attacker and one defender
(move numbers 33, 34, 35, 36, 37)

1. From left Gedan Barai the attacker steps forward with right **Oi Zuki Jodan**

2. The defender stands in Heisoku Dachi, feet together and fists together at left hip, and then steps forward into right **Zenkutsu** and **Yama Zuki**, blocking the attack and countering at the same time

3. Attacker shifts back to right Zenkutsu Dachi Gedan Barai and defender brings front foot back feet together, with both fists at the right hip. The attacker steps forward again with left **Oi Zuki Jodan**

4. The defender steps forward into left Zenkutsu and Yama Zuki, the right hand blocking the attack and countering at the same time

5. Attacker shifts back to left Zenkutsu Dachi Gedan Barai and defender brings front foot back feet together, with both fists at the left hip. From left Gedan Barai the attacker steps forward with right **Oi Zuki Jodan**

6. The defender with feet together and fists together at left hip, steps forward into right Zenkutsu and Yama Zuki, blocking the attack and countering at the same time

Defence against Oi Zuki Jodan

1. **Attacker and defender are both in left Zenkutsu Dachi position. Attacker steps forward with Oi Zuki Jodan from left Gedan Barai**

2. **Defender steps to the left with both feet together blocking with right Tate Shuto**

3. & 4. **The defender then kicks right Yoko Geri Keage Chudan and lands countering with right Yoko Empi in Kiba Dachi**

5. & 6. **From this position the defender's right foot sweeps behind the attacker's front foot with Ashi Barai. The combination is then finished with a right Gyaku Zuki**

Application for Enpi with two attackers and one defender
(move numbers 1, 2, 3, 4)

1. Attacker from left Gedan Barai takes one step forward with Oi Zuki Chudan and Gyaku Zuki Jodan

2. Defender from Enpi Yoi position, both hands on the left hip, steps to left and lowers body blocking right Gedan Barai

3. The Jodan Gyaku Zuki is blocked with right Nagashi Uke as the defender raises his body to the standing position

4. The defender stands with both fists on the left hip, ready for the second attacker on the right

5. The second attacker from the right steps forward attacking with left Mae Geri

6. The defender steps to the right and blocks the kick with right Gedan Barai

Enpi continued.....

7. The first attacker now steps forward with a left Oi Zuki Chudan

8. The defender moves the left foot back into Kiba Dachi avoiding the punch and makes a left Kage Zuki to the attacker's body

Kaishu Ippon Kumite (Attack then Block and Counter)

1. The attacker starts in left Gedan Barai position, the defender Yoi. Attacker steps forward with right Oi Zuki Jodan from left Gedan Barai

2. Defender steps back from yoi position with left Age Uke and counters with right Gyaku Zuki

3. Attacker blocks the Gyaku Zuki with left reverse Gedan Barai

4. And counters with a right Kizami Zuki Jodan keeping the left arm out as cover

Six Different Defences Against an Attacker Pushing Forward with Gyaku Zuki Chudan

1. The attacker and defender are both in Jiu Kumite Kamae position. The attacker then pushes forward with a strong Gyaku Zuki Chudan

2. The defender counters with Gyaku Zuki Jodan using fast timing and catching the attacker as he pushes forward

1. The attacker and defender are both in Jiu Kumite Kamae position. The attacker then pushes forward with a strong Gyaku Zuki Chudan

2. Defender counters with left Kizami Zuki Jodan moving to the left and outside the line of attack

1. The attacker and defender are both in Jiu Kumite Kamae position. The attacker then pushes forward with a strong Gyaku Zuki Chudan

2. Defender jumps up changing stance from left to right, countering right Kizami Zuki Jodan whilst in the air

Defences against Gyaku Zuki Chudan continued.....

1. The attacker and defender are both in Jiu Kumite Kamae position. The attacker then pushes forward with a strong Gyaku Zuki Chudan

2. Defender counters with left jodan Uraken using fast timing

3. The defender uses speed to make his counter attack before the Gyaku Zuki reaches its target

1. The attacker and defender are both in Jiu Kumite Kamae position. The attacker then pushes forward with a strong Gyaku Zuki Chudan

2. Defender covers with left Gedan Barai

3. And then counters with a right reverse Jodan Uraken Uche moving to the left

Defences against Gyaku Zuki Chudan continued.....

1. The attacker and defender are both in Jiu Kumite Kamae position. The attacker then pushes forward with a strong Gyaku Zuki Chudan

2. Defender jumps up changing stance from left to right, countering right jodan Uraken whilst off the ground

3. Defender lands in a strong Zenkutsu Dachi

4. And snaps back the Jodan Uraken counter attack

Application for Gankaku with two attackers and one defender
(move numbers 1, 2, 3, 4, 5, 6, 7, 8)

1. Attacker from left Gedan Barai takes one step forward with Oi Zuki Jodan followed by two Chudan punches

2. Defender from Yoi position steps back with the right leg into right Kokutsu Dachi blocking with a Jodan side combined block, Te Awase Uke

Application for Gankaku continued.....

3. Then lowering both hands to make **Osae Uke** to block the second punch

4. The left arm is then straightened to the front making **Uchi Zuki**, blocking the third punch

5. The defender then makes a right **Gyaku Zuki** in **Kokutsu Dachi**

6. The defender sweeps the attacker's foot away with his right foot

7. The second attacker from behind, then steps forward with a right **Oi Zuki Chudan**. The defender turns and blocks right **Gedan Barai** to the second attacker's **Oi Zuki** whilst stamping down on his foot landing in **Kiba Dachi**

8. The first attacker then steps forward with **Oi Zuki Jodan**. The defender turns and blocks **Jodan Kosa Uke**

Application for Gankaku continued.....

9. **The attacker's hand is then trapped and pulled down**

10. **With the attacker's hand trapped, the defender finishes with a right Chudan Mae Geri**

Defence Against Mawashi Geri Attack

1. **Attacker and defender both start in left Jiu Kumite Kamae position. Attacker steps forward with right Jodan Mawashi Geri**

2. **Defender moves front foot forward, lowers the hips and ducks down very low under the kick**

3. **The defender escapes behind the attacker as the kick is extended**

4. **The defender then turns towards the attacker and counters with left Chudan Gyaku Zuki**

Application for Wankan with one attacker and one defender
(move numbers 3, 4, 5, 6, 7)

1. **Attacker from left Gedan Barai steps forward with Oi Zuki Jodan. The defender is in left Kokutsu Dachi facing 45 degrees to the right**

2. **Defender from left Kokutsu Dachi brings right knee up and traps the punch with Hasami Uke pressing both wrists together to keep hold of the attack**

3. & 4. **The defender then steps forward with the right foot into right Zenkutsu Dachi and continues straightaway with another left step and then another right, pushing the attacker backwards and keeping the punching arm trapped**

5. **As the third step is made, the defender's left hand pushes Tate Shuto into the attacker's right shoulder**

6. **The defender then finishes with right Chudan Oi Zuki**

Wankan continued.....

7. **And finally left Chudan Gyaku Zuki**

Application for Meikyo with one attacker and one defender
(move numbers 31, 32, 33)

1. **The attacker who is behind the defender, steps forward with right Oi Zuki Jodan from left Gedan Bari position**

2. **Defender in Kokutsu Dachi facing away from attacker turns and blocks left Age Uke in right Kokutsu Dachi**

3. **The defender now jumps up forward and around the attacker in a triangular jump – Sankaku Tobi, using the hard part of the inside elbow to attack the head**

4. **The defender lands with a right Shuto Uke in left Kokutsu Dachi behind the attacker**

Defence using Empi Uchi with one attacker and one defender

1. The attacker starts in left Zenkutsu Dachi, the defender in Yoi position

2. The attacker steps forward with right Chudan Oi Zuki. The defender steps back blocking with right Soto Ude Uke in right Zenkutsu Dachi

3. The defender then pushes forward with a right Yoko Empi Uche in Kiba Dachi

4. The defender then adds a left Jodan Mawashi Empi in right Zenkutsu Dachi

5. And then a right Jodan Age Empi

6. The defender then steps with the left leg around to the rear of the attacker

Defence using Empi Uchi continued.....

7. As the step behind the attacker is made, the defender counters with right Ushiro Empi Uche to the back of the attacker's head

8. And finishes with left Otoshi Empi Uche to the attacker's back, pulling the opponent lower with the right hand

Defence Against Mae Geri Using Ushiro Geri Counter Attack

1. The attacker on the right is ready to kick chudan Mae Geri

2. As the attacker kicks chudan Mae Geri, the defender steps back and turns blocking with right Nagashi Uke

3. Defender lifts left heel for counter attack

4. Defender completes the counter attack with left chudan Ushiro Geri

Defence Using Front Hand Only to Block Jodan Kizami Zuki and Mawashi Geri

1. Defender on the left, ready to defend against jodan Kizami Zuki from the attacker on the right

2. Attacker pushes forward with left jodan Kizami Zuki. The defender pushes back blocking left jodan Nagashi Uke

3. The attacker brings the rear right leg forward and prepares to kick left jodan Mawashi Geri

4. The attacker's knee lifts and the kick is aimed towards the target

5. The defender pushes back once more blocking the kick with left jodan Soto Ude Uke

6. The defender finally counters with left jodan Kizami Zuki using the same arm to block and counter

Sunset –
The Legacy

GRIEF VISITED US SUDDENLY, like an unexpected and unwelcome storm. He seemed immortal, like a giant landmark from which we based all of our references.

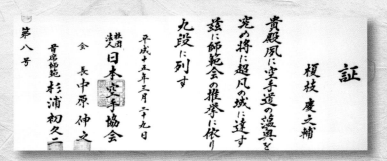

The JKA 9th Dan was posthumously awarded to Sensei Enoeda

Master Keinosuke Enoeda passed away on 29th March 2003 in Tokyo, Japan, after four months of treatment for stomach cancer. He visited Japan initially for treatment towards the end of 2002, but never made a recovery from this killer disease. The funeral was held on 21st April in Tokyo at the Hozoji Temple of JKA instructor Lida Sensei. A memorial service was also held at Crystal Palace in London on 1st June 2003. Kimihide Takechi, a Buddhist priest who is also a JKA instructor, conducted the funeral service. Karate instructors and many long-standing students from all over the world attended both the funeral in Japan and the memorial service in London. At this time a posthumous award of 9th Dan JKA was made, dated 29th March 2003. Only seven previous awards of 9th Dan have ever been made during the long history of the JKA. The award to Sensei Enoeda was the eighth.

The annual August Crystal Palace 2003 course was held as a Memorial Course in honour of Sensei Enoeda, with Sensei Ohta, Ueki, Imamura, Tomita, Matsui and Nemoto teaching on the course. Mrs Reiko Enoeda as the guest of honour also attended the course, which was full to capacity. This was the last of the special courses to be held at Crystal Palace, as the whole building and the area surrounding it are due for imminent redevelopment. Strange that so many things came to an end in 2003. The 2003 KUGB National Championships held in Birmingham, were also dedicated to the memory of Sensei Enoeda.

Ironic also that supersonic flight together with the life of Concorde also finished in the same year, starting in the 1960s and finishing in 2003, and similar in duration to the Enoeda Era. Maybe I am a fatalist in thinking this way or linking unrelated separate events,

The memorial service held at Crystal Palace on 1st June 2003

**Mrs Reiko Enoeda with the instructors
at the 2003 Crystal Palace Memorial Course**

but all the same, to me there seems some correlation between the two events, which carried both air travel, and karate forward to previously unimagined heights. The ending of flights by Concorde this year (2003), reminded me of a conversation I once had with Sensei Enoeda. We were driving in my small and cramped Toyota MR2. We saw Concorde passing over near Heathrow airport and both admired the wonderful sight above. He told me proudly how he had once travelled in Concorde to New York. His scheduled flight with British Airways to New York had been cancelled and he had been given a ticket on Concorde as compensation to complete the journey. He told me with great enthusiasm the details of the flight and the excitement that he felt travelling across the world at such great speed.

I hope that Sensei Enoeda knew and understood the effect that he had on the world of karate. I wonder whether he did. He seemed equally happy and at home teaching maybe a dozen or so students at his Marshall Street Dojo, as he did teaching maybe 500 students on an international course in America, Europe or Asia. He seemed also equally happy down the pub having a pint with a few students as he would be having a marvellous meal with a group of famous

**Mrs Reiko Enoeda with the author holding the JKA 9th
Dan certificate awarded to Sensei Enoeda**

celebrities. He totally enjoyed his life and his time spent with the people who he knew and also thought a lot of. I remember one day asking him just what was the greatest benefit that he had gained during his many years of teaching karate. He replied simply, "Friends – I have met so many wonderful friends. Real and lasting friendship is worth more than gold or diamonds." He looked me in the eye and smiled as we drank a toast. "To friends!"

He was also extremely generous. On one occasion when I was assisting him in moving home I admired one of his valuable personal items. He would not let me leave without taking it with me. On this particular occasion my job was to assist in helping him move all of his own important items into his small personal study room. We carried all of the boxes, drawers and the small amount of furniture up to the top floor and into his room. I could see that the bulk of the items that we carried into the room were books, karate books, dozens and dozens of them. We lined them up neatly on the shelves around the room and when we finished Sensei Enoeda stood back and smiled with satisfaction. On this day I saw a different person to whom I had ever seen before. I saw Enoeda the student of karate, someone who loved the art so much he wanted to be immersed in it and continually research and learn from the prized collection of books that surrounded him. As well as being a great teacher I believe he was also a great student of karate. The legacy of Sensei Enoeda is huge. Apart from the books and videos that he made, there are the classes, courses and lessons that those who were lucky enough to train with him remember so well. The thousands of competitors that he trained up to international level and who inspired many others to begin karate. Most of all, the legacy of the instructors whom he took under his wing to give that bit of special help and advice. These instructors will carry forward Enoeda's teachings to future generations of karate students and try to pass them on. There are lots of them – from all over the world. Indeed, it was Sensei Enoeda's skill that made EVERYONE who he came into contact with feel unique and special, especially the instructors.

In 2003, when Sensei Enoeda passed away, I felt driven to set up a *Book of Condolence* on the Internet. The karate world was in shock. Nobody could actually believe what had happened. Many messages came to me via the telephone and email from all quarters requesting information as to how, why and what had happened. Dojo all over the world were silent in respect for the Master. Eventually these requests for information turned to messages of sympathy, which was when the virtual *Book of Condolence* was launched on the Internet.

I was so touched by some of the beautiful tributes that were written, I thought they should be given to the family of Sensei Enoeda. And so it was that towards the end of 2003, Steve Bere, one of Sensei's students, and I had the book professionally bound and presented to Mrs Reiko Enoeda. A few of these written tributes appear below, with kind thanks to all of the contributors.

Harry Wilson

I would just like to give my condolences to Sensei K. Enoeda's family and his loyal secretary Chieko, who has worked with Sensei for many years, also Sensei Ohta who I'm sure has everybody's full support. I have been very fortunate to train under Sensei K.Enoeda from 7th kyu to 3rd dan over 20 to 25 years at Marshall St. It has come as a great shock to hear of his sad passing. I'm confident his spirit will live on inside all his loyal students who have trained under him during the many years he dedicated to Shotokan karate in the UK and beyond. Thank you Sensei. Harry Wilson 3rd Dan JKA

Alexander Farmer

I would like to sign my name - Alexander Farmer, from the Eton College dojo – in the book for condolences for Sensei Enoeda. Sensei was my great-

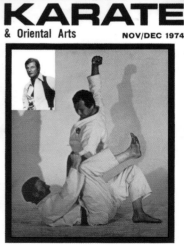

No. 51   35p

est inspiration in karate... He inspired in me a deep desire to excel in karate, uphold all its principals and be a good karate-ka. I miss his great character and his teaching very, very much. Thank you so much for what you gave me Sensei. Domo origato gozaimashita. Karate Ni Sente Nashi.

Tim Kiel USA

I am very sorry to hear of the passing of Mr. Enoeda, I was only able to train under him in one class, but he is someone I have admired and respected for the past 30 years. A legend in his time. Our thoughts and prayers go to his family and loved ones. Thank you. Sincerely, Sensei Tim Kiel and students, Central Minnesota Karate, USA

Kasajima Keichi Luxembourg

Cher ami, Quelle triste nouvelle, la mort de sensei Enoeda. Sinceres condoleances, mais nous allons continuer dans la voie de Sensei. Kasajima Keiichi

Robert Sidoli - Canada

The karate world has lost a truly great man. Regardless of political affiliation I am sure that has been an inspiration to millions of karate-ka world-wide. He will be sadly missed. I hope that he realised what impact he truly had on the karate world, and just how much he was appreciated. My deepest condolences go to his wife and children, the SKC and his many students. I was in Japan whilst Enoeda Sensei was ill. I heard of his illness whilst on the train to Tokyo. I can assure you all that many people in Japan (other than JKA) were concerned about him. All spoke extremely well of him. The respect he held is colossal. He was one of the last of the true JKA legends. Robert Sidoli Karatenomichi Sekai Renmei

Derek Bier

Sensei Enoeda You inspired me to go beyond my Kyu grade and attain Dan status. Always proud but with a hint of humour I remember you clearly at one of my first Crystal Palace courses. I was a 1st Kyu unable to Mawashi Geri. As you proceeded down the line I was in, you stood in front of me and made it perfectly clear I needed to complete this kick or else! For the first time in my life I saw my foot appear in front of my body at head level! Thank you for 30 years of Karate, which has brought me fitness, a clear mind, peace and happiness

Barbara Thurston

I am very sorry to hear of Sensei Enoeda's death. It was a privilege to have attended his courses. He always conducted himself with dignity, humility and not a little humour. He will be sadly missed but widely and fondly remembered by many people who hardly knew him. Thoughts and blessings go to his family and friends.

Gerald Wagner - Holland

Karate has lost one of his greatest masters. I had the privilege to learn Karate in a small dojo in Amsterdam founded by two of Sensei Enoeda's students. His spirit was always with us and will stay with us.

Maureen Gordon

It is difficult to find the right words at a time like this. I would like to offer my sympathies to all karate-ka and to the family of Sensei Enoeda. It is a comfort to share the sense of loss with other people. I will never forget everything this wonderful man did for my karate and he will continue to live in my heart and in my memories. Good night Sensei.

Ljupco Apcevski - Budokwai

Boss, I miss you!

Lucy Traettino - Chingford

My sincere condolences go to the family of Sensei Enoeda. One of my most treasured memories of Sensei Enoeda will be when we took him for dinner one evening after he had attended our club for a

course and grading and he asked me to pick something for him to eat. It was an opportunity to see the man behind the karate suit, just enjoying a meal and chatting away. He was a truly great man and Master of Karate. I will miss him but never forget him. Lucy

Nirmal Perera

Very sad to hear about the loss of one of the true legends of modern day Karate. He certainly was an inspiration to us all. My own instructor who is a direct student of Sensei Enoeda talked about him endlessly, sometimes in the middle of lessons and he certainly seemed to have earned a lot of respect from his students. It was no surprise however when I saw him. I remember training with him a few times at his Crystal Palace seminars. I remember watching him demonstrate and he was so good he could take your breath away. He was about sixty yet he moved like a thirty year old, a phenomenal athlete right till the end. It is certainly an honour knowing that I have trained with and have been graded by one of the truly great Karate Masters and I am very proud to wear his belt. Sensei Enoeda you were and still are the greatest. You inspired generations of people and you'll go on inspiring more. Many respects. Oss Sensei

Jim Wood MBE and Aileen – Scotland JKA

Words cannot describe the pain I feel at this time with the loss of a dear friend and mentor. I will be travelling to Japan this week to say a fond farewell. My deepest sympathy goes out to all who knew and loved him, and in particular to his family, especially Mrs Enoeda, who allowed us to share time and wonderful memories with her husband for over 33years. His spirit will be with us at Crystal Palace in May. Sayonara Sensei!

Bengal School of Shotokan - India.

May you have the strength to bear this loss. I was so unfortunate in this regard. I never got to meet the Great master. I am so upset along with my students. We had such great respect and regard for him. One of his students is a Sensei in our dojo. Onu Jaigidar, On behalf of all of us we send our heartfelt condolences to the whole karate family. Please keep in touch with us we will definitely meet in the future. Shihan Enoeda will always be in our thoughts and we will miss him. I just do not have words good enough to tell you exactly how I feel. This is one of the greatest losses of all the Shotokan Karateka. He will live in our thoughts and we will keep him alive in the art. Please accept this gesture from us we extend our love, respect and prayers for all. Bengal School of Shotokan. Dhaka, Bangladesh

Deddy Mansyur – USA

Very sad news to hear that our great Sensei Enoeda is no longer with us. I am sure he is in a better 'dojo' now, knowing the good things he did for us to perfect our karate-do. I sure do miss him. He was a legend. He had a sense of humour. Let's keep our karate-do spirit alive and continue to teach our students to do the right things in karate-do. We always start with the dojo-kun and practice them every day. Oss! deddy mansyur UH-Shotokan Karate-Do

Onu Jaigirdar – India

I feel deeply the loss of a revered Sensei. A leader by example, with a spirit that shone loud into our hearts. He imbued us with pride, a sense of belonging, and a natural balance. He may have left us behind, but his teaching and spirit will live on through us, his students. Our thoughts are also with his family during this time of grieving. ONU JAIGIRDAR Dhaka Bangladesh

Jose Luis Silva

Foi com espanto e admiração que soube da morte do Sensei Enoeda, por isso, e porque sempre o admirei, lamento profundamente a sua morte e em particular a falta da referência que o estágio do Crystal Palace tinha com o seu nome e a sua presença. Mas o seu desaparecimento físico não implicará o seu desaparecimento definitivo porque os grandes mestres nunca morrem estando sempre presentes nos nossos corações e nas nossas mentes. Bem hajas Sensei Enoeda por tudo o que fizeste pelo Karate mundial e por eu ter tido o previlégio de ter sido graduado à muitos anos atrás para 2° Dan pela tua pessoa... Oss Enoeda Sensei.

Simon Marchant-Jones

Sensei Enoeda's memory will live on. I'll never forget his visits to Leeds for gradings in the late 70's when I first started training with Bob Rhodes, and how his charisma filled the dojo. In 1979 I came to London and joined Marshall Street, where we had the great privilege of regular instruction from Sensei Enoeda and his family's company on holidays in Spain. He had a great sense of fun especially when we all demanded a song from him at social events. My sincere condolences go to his family at their sad loss of such a great man at such an early age.

Bob and Jill Edwards

We send our condolences to the family of Sensei K. Enoeda. We are very proud to have had the opportunity to meet, train and be inspired by one of the greatest representatives of the JKA He will be sadly missed. Tamari K.C. Co. Durham

Gilbert A. Bodley – British Virgin Islands

Sincere condolences to the family, friends and students of the revered and great Sensei K. Enoeda, on behalf of family and myself. Our prayers are with you. Your sadness is our sadness, and hope that Joy will return to all our hearts soon. It was a pleasure and memorable occasion to attend a few of his sessions at the annual Camp Greenlane, in Philadelphia, USA a couple years ago, where we were all inspired by this great Shihan. His "Spirit" will forever continue to lead us. Farewell Great One, and may the Great Architect lead you to that new and better world. OSSSUU. (British Virgin Islands)

Mark Ringwaldt – Australia

To Mrs Reiko Enoeda, her children Daisuke, Maya and their respective families, I send my condolences to you all. It seems that legends and great men live on forever, but unfortunately as human beings we don't. However Sensei Enoeda's spirit and inspiration will live on through those people who were privileged to have been touched or inspired by him. Osu. Mark Ringwaldt Hobart, Tasmania, Australia.

Florence Hands – JKA Oasis – Budokwai

My deepest sympathy to Mrs Enoeda and her family for the terrible loss of Sensei Enoeda. I realise how fortunate I have been to be able to train with sensei Enoeda in Marshall Street and I am very grateful to him for everything he taught me. I will carry on training remembering all those fantastic moments and I will do my best to pass on the good spirit and the tradition of karate, as he wanted it to be. He will always be present in my heart. Florence Hands (JKA / Oasis-Budokwai)

John Teo Song Chew – Singapore

Deepest condolences and heartfelt sadness to Sensei Enoeda's family, friends and students at the passing of a great Shotokan karate teacher. It was way back in 1968 that I was fortunate enough to

be able to train under Sensei Enoeda, whenever he would come down to Portsmouth KUGB Shotokan karate club to conduct lessons. There were Sensei Kanazawa and Takahashi as well, all based in London. It was a grand era then as Shotokan karate was spreading rapidly all over UK and Europe. The students were of very great dedication and the Sensei then were in their physical prime. It was a real treat and very inspiring to watch them demonstrating advanced techniques and katas on the special occasions. May Sensei Enoeda rest in everlasting peace. How the years have passed and yet it seem like only yesterday.

Tony Aidoo – Chingford and Wanstead

It is with the deepest sadness that I write this small tribute to the late Sensei Enoeda. A big void has been left which, in my opinion, will never be filled in the grand art of shotokan karate. I have been very privileged to train with Sensei Enoeda on numerous occasions; club courses (Chingford & Wanstead), special summer courses at Crystal Palace, England senior squad training and also as a competitor with him as a referee. His presence is always felt from within. The whole Shotokan karate Associations over the entire world will miss him dearly; my heartfelt thoughts and condolences go to his family and friends. Oss.

Mirjam "Miss Swiss" Widmer - Switzerland

Dear Sensei, I miss you! With sadness I heard what had happened. I have no words to express my feelings. But I have memories deep in my heart of a great time, training at Marshall Street, with you, feeling the spirit and power! - It was a great time. It was a great experience for every karateka. We all will keep on training the way you where teaching us and carry on feeling your spirit. Respectfully I would like to send my sincere condolence to Enoeda Sensei's family.

Majo Xeridat

Sensei Enoeda has always been a legend. It is hard to believe he is no more. I look back on all the hours I spent training under him either at Marshall Street or at Crystal Palace and can't imagine that such a strong spirit can just stop. Meeting some of the old crowd the other day I could see the legacy in them. He has touched so many of us that we can never let him go from our soul. My sincere condolences to his family both at home and in Karate.

Michelle Jenkinson - Manchester

Having graded and trained with Sensei Enoeda for over 27 years, we have been truly blessed to meet a wonderful man and an inspiration to all. May he rest in peace and watch over his beloved family. Much sympathy to Mrs Enoeda and her family, he was a great man. I feel very honoured to have met him. Michelle Jenkinson, Manchester, England

Mike Gardner -London

Almost 20 years ago, I started training with Sensei at Marshall Street. I am very lucky to have spent my whole training life with him and Ohta Sensei. The feeling of his sessions were mixed with fear and awe. I have been very lucky enough to work with him on his Crystal Palace Course for the last 15 years. This next May course will be very hard as his presence was so great. I also need to say goodbye to him with all my friends who have been coming to Crystal Palace over the years, not only to Enoeda Sensei but also his great friend Tabata Sensei who will also be sorely missed. May at Crystal Palace will be very different without these two masters. Oss Sensei

Nick Heald

Goodbye to a great man. Sensei Enoeda was an inspiration to thousands and he will be missed terribly. Whilst I would have loved our team (Leeds) to have won the 2003 Nationals, it seemed somehow fitting that Sensei's team won this year. Well done lads, I'm sure he was cheering you on!

Paul and Maria McDonnell Staff – Australia

We were very privileged and proud to have trained at Marshall Street SKC and to have known Sensei Enoeda as more than our instructor, along with many others. He was a great man who was instrumental in taking Karate out from Japan to the world, in particular Europe, and especially the UK through the KUGB. His accomplishments speak for themselves, but we would like to put on record a different side to Sensei and pay tribute to his warmth as a human being, his generosity, his wicked sense of humour and his dry wit, his smile and his deep booming laugh. He was a man who enjoyed life and in many ways epitomised the Karate ideal. His example was an absolute inspiration to thousands of students, not just those of the KUGB. All will mourn him deeply. Through his students, his philosophy both in respect of karate and life will live on, and what better legacy can one leave? Sayonara, Sensei

Paul Herbert

As part of the winning team, I would just like to take this opportunity to dedicate SKC Budokwai's victory in the KUGB National Championships to the inspiration behind us all - Sensei Keinosuke Enoeda That was for you Sensei – Oss

David and Wendy Osborne – JKA Scotland

We both feel a great loss at the passing of Sensei Enoeda and we wish to pass our sincere condolences to his wife and family. My wife and I have attended many courses in Scotland and attained all our grades from him over the past 25 years. His karate is our karate. Long may his legacy carry on.

Einar Hagen – Norway

My condolences to the family of Sensei Enoeda. I feel very grateful to have been able to train with him on many occasions. He will be remembered fondly for a very long time at the JKA Norway honbu dojo.

Gary Stewart – London

In a squad training session at Marshall St, Roy Cudjoe once put my nose across the other side of my face with a (lucky) Mawashi geri. Enoeda Sensei folded a towel and pushed it back again. Sensei stood back and was lining my nose up like an artist, until he was pleased with the outcome. Onlookers looked on squeamishly but I had been told to stand still, so I did. I have twenty-one years of great memories with Enoeda Sensei. Well done to the Budokwai team in winning the Nationals, you know how much that title meant to him.

B.Rani Padamsee – India

Please accept our heartfelt condolences. It is one of my greatest losses not having met the Great Master. I had visited his dojo twice but in vain. I am really sad and upset at this great loss for all the Karateka who could have benefited endlessly from his knowledge and superb teaching abilities. We pray for his departed soul and our hope is that his family, students and friends have the courage to bear this pain and loss and keep him alive by continuing his good work. I will visit the dojo whenever I am in London and feel his spirit there. I am sure he will live forever with the wonderful things he has done and the able family and students he has left behind. My very best to everyone and may Allah give all of us the courage and ability to live up to his expectations. May the spirit of karatedo live forever and ever..........From Bangladesh with love

Dermot O'Keeffe – Ireland

Deeply saddened at Sensei Enoeda's passing. It was always an exciting time for me when he visited Ireland. He will be missed by my fellow students and me.

Mike and Ruth Dosh

It's hard at times like this to realise that someone you thought was invincible was human after all, Enoeda Sensei was our biggest role model and the world of Shotokan Karate is a lot poorer without him. Knowing Sensei since 1986 was one of the best things that could have happened to Ruth and I. Enoeda Sensei gave us the inspiration to continue training, as we grow older and to strive for excellence in all we do. We send our heartfelt sympathies to Enoeda Sensei's family for their loss. God bless you. Mike & Ruth Dosh and all the students at Houghton Sendai & Hokkaido Karate Clubs.

Kaida Takamori

Sensei- au koto ga arimasen... totemo zannen desu. au koto ga arimasen kedo honto ni itsumo o'sewa ni narimashita yo- sensei no koto ha sekai kara itsumo narau dekimasu ne. Sensei, arigatoo.

Stephen F. Krauss – USA

I had the pleasure of living in London and Liverpool in 1966-67 during which time I founded the University of Liverpool Karate Club. I trained with Enoeda Sensei whenever I had a chance, and I saw him in the States as well. Talking with him over dinner or just while we were walking, gave me some insight into his personality. He left a strong impression, and I have spoken often about him to other karateka. I found his Shotokan Advanced Kata series of books well done and recommended them to students. I was surprised and saddened to hear of his passing. I give my heartfelt condolences to his family and to the KUGB family as well. Best wishes to all. Stephen F. Krauss, Denver, Colorado USA.

Luis Pereira – Portugal

I would like to pay my respects to a Great Master of Shotokan Karate. My sympathy goes as well to his family and friends. Sensei Enoeda we will miss you. REST IN PEACE. Luís Pereira from Portugal

Ian Balt – South Africa

I can with out a doubt say we've lost a great teacher and friend. I really feel when I say all Shotokan clubs in South Africa will miss him and he will live in our mind, body and spirit forever. OSSU 'TIGER'

David Isenberg – USA

Enoeda Sensei was once a guest instructor at the annual summer camp the ISKF holds in Green lane, Pennsylvania. Suffice it to say that even though I trained with him for a small amount of time he was obviously every bit the master that he was said to be. Just being in his presence was inspirational.

Touati

C'est avec une profonde tristesse que j'ai appris la disparition de Sensei K.Enoeda.je tiens à le remercier pour son enseignement et sa gentillesse. C'est avec lui et les sensei Shirai, Kasé et Myazaki que j'ai tout appris du karaté. Sincères condoléances à sa famille et ses amis.

Douglas Walsh – USA

I was very shocked and saddened when I heard that Master Keinosuke Enoeda had passed away on March 29, 2003. Not too long ago, I had heard that he had been sick, but that he was recovering and expected to return to England. Knowing his strong spirit and fortitude, it seemed he would certainly make a full recovery. As are the many that knew him and trained under him, I too, remain in shock. Master Enoeda was an outstanding teacher and motivator. We, in the US always looked forward to his visits and classes. He always pushed us in his classes go beyond our limits and motivated us to do what we often thought we could not do. He set the example for us to follow. Not only his classes, but his many books, videos and articles were (and still

are) inspiring and very helpful. Even in these, one can sense and feel his enormous spirit! I feel very lucky to have had the opportunity to train under and meet the great man in both the UK and the US We all will miss Master Enoeda. But his spirit will live on! God Bless you Sensei. Sincerely, Douglas Walsh JKA/ISKF Southern Region USA

Graham Richardson

I have been a member of Marshall St. SKC for 25 years, which is half my life! Not to hear and see Enoeda Sensei in the Dojo is very hard. But he lives on in all our hearts. He has changed the lives of us all in some way, in and out of the Dojo. One Night after training about 2 years ago I was sitting with James Marshall in the pub, Enoeda Sensei

came in and sat with us and asked why I had not been training as much lately. I told him that as I was getting older it was getting harder etc. to train. He explained that when he was 55 years old it was painful to train, but he carried on. Then at 60 he thought the same, but carried on, now he was 65 he felt so good that he was glad that he carried on training. He made promise that I would train least once per week, if not he said I would lose the 'feeling'. It is a great loss to us all, and we must keep up his style of Shotokan and not lose the 'feeling.' Condolences to all family and friends. Thank you Sensei for everything, "just one more time" Oss. Graham Richardson.

Hashem Zafarani – Kilburn

When I heard the sad news of Sensei K.Enoeda passing away I didn't really have any emotion. But when I thought about it afterwards I realised that a big chunk of my life had been taken out! Sensei K. Enoeda had a VERY big impact on my life because I had graded under him up until my 2nd Dan. When I did not pass my 2nd Dan and I only had got kumite only I had felt that I was not very good but my Sensei, Sensei Eric Pich came up to me and said "He didn't pass your kumite because he was so impressed by the rest of your grading." When I heard that news I was so determined to pass the next time. The next time I did pass and I was so impressed because I proved to Sensei that I could pass. Also on one of the Crystal Palace courses when I was a 1st kyu I was in the front line and Sensei K.Enoeda was walking up and down talking and he stopped in front of me and I thought "Oh no what have I done wrong?" He looked down at me and gave me a smile and he fixed my belt because I had tied it wrong. He told me to stand up and he fixed it for me, I bowed and said OSS and went back into front stance. I felt like he cared for me. I recently went up for squad selection and got on and I had hoped for the next training session for Sensei K.Enoeda to teach because I heard that he had taught before. But now that he has gone. Whenever I train I shall always see Sensei K.Enoeda in my mind! My condolences to Sensei K.Enoeda family and we must all train with all our heart because he is watching over us. Hashem Zafarani 14yrs 2nd Dan.

Richard Barrett

I first trained with Enoeda Sensei at Marshall Street Baths in the early 70s. Not long after this I entered the southern area championship at Seymour Baths as a non-graded white belt. I was picked for the second team and ended up in the A team for the final against Thames Karate Club. We won the event. This day I will always remember as I got my first gold medal and when I received it from Enoeda Sensei he just laughed and shook his head! He will always be remembered as he helped to make Karate as it is today. Gone but never to be forgotten.

Noel Casey, B.O'Reagan, K.Murphy, M.Keohane – Ireland

We are all deeply shocked and saddened by the death of our chief instructor and a friend, Sensei K. Enoeda. Sensei's untimely passing has left a sore emptiness not only in our karate, but also in our personal lives. It is our full intention to echo Sensei's word and to ensure Ireland will continue to practice karate as a Master once thought. The spirit of the 'Tiger' will forever remain. Thank you Sensei. Oss RIP Noel Casey, Barry O'Regan, Kevin Murphy, Mick Keohane: ISKA / JKA

Shotokan Kyokai Berlin, Clubleaders Schinck and Birkholz – Germany

We were deeply saddened of the death of our great master Enoeda Keinosuke Shihan. We would like to express our sincere condolences. We all thinking of him for all the times as the best of the best. He lives on in our hearts.

Julian R. Williams – Malawi

On behalf of all students of Shotokan Karate in Malawi, please accept our heart-felt condolences. Sensei never met us and we only knew him through books and film. His influence on the development of Karate in this small country, although indirect, remains real and lasting. Sayonara, Sensei

Saripton Ming Thanarat

I started karate out of curiosity a couple of years ago at the Eton College Karate Club. At the end of the first month, there was a special training session where this Japanese dude came and taught. Sensei Enoe-who? Whatever, I gathered off the grape vine that he's some hotshot guy from Japan. As I sat at the back of the dojo in my T-shirt and tracksuit bottoms and watched him, silenced screamed in my ears shutting out my friend's shuffling and someone else's coughing; irrelevance rendered everything else to disappear into darkness; all I saw was a man shining in the dark through his aura; all I heard was the friction on his clothes; all I knew was that I wanted to aspire to as close as I could get to this man. Soon after, I ordered my very own gi and fashioned a shining white belt. I trained very hard, only looking forward to the next special training session, wanting to show him what I had learnt. As I found out more and more from the higher belts who Enoeda Sensei was, I couldn't but help feel irrelevant myself. As the next special training approached, I gave up my little fantasy of showing him what I had learnt and telling him how much of an inspiration he was to me. Who am I? Why does he even come to our club that consists of two black belts, a handful of middle grades, and a couple of T-shirt wearers. Man, what a waste of time it must be to come and teach us when he could be training up the advanced black belts. As the training session went on, I was more and more surprised. The care he took with me. The care he took with everyone. The personal details he went into with each of us. He wasn't there just to command us for 2 hours and leave. He cared and wanted to see us do it right. After the session, he went and got changed and came back out to talk to us. There was no hurry to leave, no "OK I've finished the lesson, got to go." He stayed and talked; talked about anything, about my problems he picked out during the session that I should work on, about my trip to Japan, about him inviting our club over to dinner some time. Now, there are probably thousands of stories like this. I am one of a large number of "small fish". We all have our experiences about how Sensei personally touched our lives. Each of us, despite being "small fish", claim a connection to him, claim that he is a big part of our karate. Who are we to claim this? The problem is, that is not the question. The solution is the question, "Who was he?" It doesn't matter what small fish we are, the point is that HE was able to make US feel special. There wasn't a single white belt or T-shirt wearer who was too insignificant to him. He was able to personally touch so many lives, whether they were national competitors, club instructors, or a green belt struggling from mid-rank crisis. The thousands of stories from us small fish, recounting how he did this for us and how we met him and talked to him and learnt so much and how he was our inspiration etc, is none but pure testimony to the achievements, love, respect, kindness and understanding this great, great man had. I say no more but only thank you, and good-bye, our most dear Sensei. Saritpon Ming Thanarat JKA of Stanford University 3rd April 2003

Peter Lindsay – Canada

In the world of martial arts, regardless of style, few great Masters ever emerge. Those of us who train in the art of Shotokan Karate can take great pride in the fact that Enoeda Sensei was one of the few. Living here in Canada I never had the privilege of training with Enoeda Sensei and any influence he may have had on the development of my karate was only pictorial in nature, none the less the quality of his karate and his love for the art of Shotokan was clearly evident on every page and in every movement. My deepest sympathies go out to his family, and too all of his students throughout the world. I hope that your memories of his life and all that he gave to the development of Shotokan Karate will be of some comfort to you today, and in the years to come. Sensei Peter Lindsay on behalf of all of the students at Westshore Karate, Victoria, BC, Canada.

Ken Fanner – ISKA

Sensei Enoeda will be greatly missed by all at I.S.K.A (GB), Sensei Ray Vout, Sensei Mim Vout, Sensei Glen Hall, & Sensei Ken Fanner all who have trained under Sensei Enoeda ion the past 30 years. Ray and Mim Vout were Southern Secretary with the KUGB up to '96 and had a personal connection with Sensei Enoeda. He will be greatly missed by us all and will leave a vast void in not only Shotokan

Karate, but also the martial arts world. I believe that his era in which he guided us all in Shotokan karate should by named after him. Rest in Peace, Sensei Enoeda from all your students.

David Clarke – Barbados

The karate world has lost a great man with an exceptional spirit. I had the pleasure of training with Sensei Enoeda many times. He and his wonderful family visited Barbados in 1987. A trip the whole karate family in Barbados remembers with pleasure and fond memories. On behalf of all the ISKF/JKA karate family in the Caribbean, we express our sincere condolences to his family.

Dave Paulus

When I first started training at 6 years of age, the other members of my club would always talk about Enoeda Sensei. In the twenty years that followed, I

have only been fortunate enough to train with Enoeda Sensei on a few occasions. Each time he inspired me to push myself that bit further and I left every one of his lessons truly motivated to improve and try harder. I was lucky enough to train at the JKA Honbu Dojo in March 2002 and I can still remember the look on the various Instructor's faces when they saw Enoeda Sensei's signature in my licence, they had nothing but respect and admiration for him and I was proud to belong to his organisation. Shotokan Karate will not be the same without him. Rest in Peace Sensei.

Chris Spendlove

I consider myself very privileged to have met Sensei Enoeda san and to have trained under his guidance when I took up Karate in 1985. His presence dominated the Dojo the moment he walked in and those in the Dojo realised that we were all in the presence of a Great Man. I have never met anyone with more passion in the way they teach. I remember when I took my 1st Dan at Slough in 1987. He was judging the sparing part of the grading. I took a hit to the head and Sensei Enoeda san called me over to the table to see if I was hurt. "Are you alright, yes?" he asked, I replied "Yes Sensei, I'm OK" (eagerly bowing!) "You alright to continue?" he asked again, "Yes Sensei, Thank you" (still bowing a lot!). He then smiled at me and laughing as he spoke, he said "Next time get out of way, no hit to head!" I couldn't help but laugh as I bowed and went back to my line and went on to get my 1st Dan. I can still see his smiling face looking back at me after saying that to this day! It was then I realised that even a great man such as himself could still have a great sense of humour and use it to full effect. The nickname he had, Tiger, was very well deserved and still is a very fine and fitting tribute to a very much respected and influential man who touched and inspired all of those who met him. My deepest condolences to his family on the loss of a truly wonderful man.

Robert Steggles

We should all take the time to reflect on the impression he made on our lives and what he has done for Karate. We are the lucky ones would have had the privilege to have trained with him. Everyone from JKA Scotland will miss him forever. He never frightened me he only ever made me feel better and bigger! Myself and my students deepest sympathies to Reiko, Daisuke & Maya and Ohta Sensei. "What we do in life echoes in eternity."

Jacobus Malan – Wanstead

Sensei Enoeda was the one Sensei that I wanted to train with but never had the chance to. My

instructors in South Africa have trained with him and spoke with high regard about Sensei Enoeda. I have recently started training in England and the sad passing is felt deeply in the dojo I train in. All the articles and books I read and especially the pictures of him show that he was a true master. My best to the Enoeda family. We must now persist to train even harder and let Sensei Enoeda's spirit live on.

Chris Lafbury – Chingford

When I heard of the terrible news, it was one of those things that seemed somehow unreal. I have trained with Sensei Enoeda many times and met with him socially several times too. My most vivid memory of him was while I was struggling to achieve my Shodan grading. I was on a course at Crystal Palace as a brown belt and he had shown us a complicated piece of kata application for Kanku Dai. We were practising this in groups of three. By some miracle, I was able to do it well. As he walked around watching us, he looked at me and said gruffly 'very good'. He then made me demonstrate it in front of the whole class. I was very proud to have apparently pleased him. He was a great man and an inspiration to us all. He will be sadly missed.

Hugh Achilles

It was with enormous sadness that I learned of Sensei Enoeda's passing when I was sent "The Times" obituary last March. It was news that was so shocking – such an energetic and vibrant person – so unexpected. It has left me stunned. I was a very keen 13-yr-old when Rob Pons and I began training with Sensei Kanazawa back in 1966 at the Budokwai. Sensei Enoeda took over from him shortly after that and took us through many gruelling training sessions, pushing us to the extreme all the time, so that it paid off with our team winning the European Junior Champs and following with many successful British Championships. When Sensei graded me, I was the youngest Shotokan black belt ever in the UK. My memories are brimming over and there are too many incidents I could relate here. I will only tell one: It was one of our training sessions at Crystal Palace. The manager of CP was never a popular man and because of a few harsh words the night before, Rob and I proceeded to 'jam' the juke box in the recreation room on the ground floor of the accommodation block. We manually lifted the juke box through the glass doors and placed it outside where it faced the training block. We started it up and jammed it on 'Doin the Funky Chicken' very loudly. Once our 2 hour session started with Enoeda, somebody opened the windows of the dojo and just as we were all about to bow to Sensei the whole place began to be blasted with Funky Chicken. Sensei's eyes concentrated on Rob and I all through the session and we managed to avert his stares! The following morning at 6 o'clock we were rudely awoken by Andy Sherry's orders over the loudspeakers to get out of bed. Rob and I were forced to run barefoot twice around the racing car circuit, followed by a couple of circuits of the Astroturf – needless to say, Enoeda was highly amused at our sore, bleeding feet and fell about laughing for a considerable time. It was very evident that Sensei was always backed by his extremely devoted wife whom I am privileged to have met on numerous occasions. Although Rob is no longer with us either, I know he would have shared my condolences to Mrs Enoeda for all the support she gave him in those days when they lived in Richmond.

Mauricio Quesada O. – Costa Rica

I never got the chance to meet Master Enoeda because we here in Costa Rica are really far away from any of these famous Masters. Although, I can say that his books and videos are more than an inspiration to anybody that practices Shotokan Karate, and also for those who are new to the Art. I can only say that from all the students at our dojo, we are sending our very deep condolences to the family and all those who knew him well and had the chance to train with him. May God keep his soul in a special place, together with the other Masters, such as Funakoshi, Nakayama, etc. Mi más sentido pésame y saludos desde Costa Rica...

Jim Wilson

Sensiei Enoeda was carved from the rock that makes legends. My first meeting with him was back in the mid sixties at the Budokwai. I was the senior grade in a long line of eager young karate students. Sensei was walking the line and making corrections, then he stopped to look at me for a moment and without warning let loose his devastatingly powerful reverse punch, just stopping a whisker from my chin. His power was awesome, his spirit bursting with energy and his control absolute....the perfect technique....just like Sensei Enoeda.....the perfect teacher.

Tony Welsh

Cricket hall, downstairs at Crystal Palace - Friday morning. We have all been there. Three hours - floor like the surface of a table tennis bat! Anyway that's not my story. "BIG NED" as we know the legend north of the border, has left me with many memories. I would like to share two of them with my fellow karateka.
1. 1982 - Barr Head, Scotland - another terrific big Ned course. My friend Tommy Coyle asks me during one of Sensei Enoeda's explanations, "What is a weasel?" I tell him "It's a small furry animal that looks like a stoat." "Why Tommy?" I ask. He says "Ned keeps saying;

WEASEL BREATHING!" Nearly ended myself laughing.

2. 1986 - 2nd dan grading Edinburgh Scotland. Enoeda Sensei taking the grading. Kumite next, no problem me against Sensei SHINA............... (2 TIMES ALL JAPAN CHAMPION), all 18 stone of him. Sparring away I hear Enoeda Sensei say, "Tony score a point!" No bother sensei – I think. Ashi barai Kizami Zuki. The crowd gasp Oooohhhhh! That's the last thing I remember! I woke up with Enoeda Sensei slapping the soles of my feet. Later he tells me I have the spirit of a tiger. All I can say is, Sensei must have seen a lot of sleeping tigers in his day. DOMO ARIGATO SENSEI.

Mariko Watanabe

Precious moments: When I visited Enoeda-sensei in the hospital on that Saturday evening in March, I sat by his bed and placed my hand on top of his. He looked at me, lifted his oxygen mask slightly, and said "tsumetai". It was only then that I realized my hand was freezing cold. I quickly put my hand under my armpit to warm it and told him, "I've got a warm heart". He turned his head toward me and favoured me with that cunning smile of approval he always gave to his students as he watched their spirited sparring and listened to their kiai. Each time he started to drift off to sleep, I watched him and listened to his breathing. His Adam's apple slowly rose and fell as he drew each precious breath, using all his remaining strength to fill his lungs to capacity. He seemed to me to be practicing and reviewing all the kata one by one, or doing his favourite kata for the last time. At times he could hardly keep his eyes open, but his mind remained as sharp as a tiger's claw. At times I didn't think he was listening, but he responded every time. I never had to repeat myself, and if he disapproved of what I said, he signalled his displeasure by moving his index finger from side to side. Before I left that evening, we thumb wrestled for a while. Somehow I thought I would win, but despite his weight loss he was surprisingly strong. I lost! As I stood up to leave, I said to sensei, "I will see you tomorrow morning," and he replied with a 'thumbs up'. It was a little before 8:30p.m. on March 29th, 2003. Sometime during the next few hours he was gone forever in the physical sense, but he lives on in the memory of some of the most precious moments I spent with Enoeda-sensei, The Tiger. Rest in Peace.

Yasurakani... Mariko.

Mrs Reiko Enoeda with the author

The words of tribute to Sensei Enoeda on these last few pages have come from all over the world and emphasise just how great his impact was on so many people's lives. Far from being "left alone at sea", there is an overriding will to keep the legacy of Sensei Enoeda alive and to maintain the skills and standards that he has given us. For his sake and for the sake of karate we must all aim to do just that.

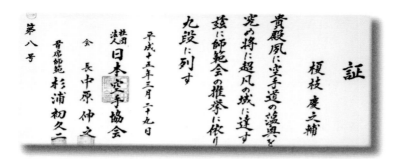

JKA Dan Grades

Shodan (1st Dan)

This level necessitates the motivation of all basic body movements and techniques, including hand and leg techniques to be applied with extended force and proper application in basic combinations.

Nidan (2nd Dan)

This stage requires the personal assimilation and performance of all basic body movements and techniques to such a degree that their application is in accord with the individual's own unique body demands.

Sandan (3rd Dan)

Has acquired the understanding of the underlying principles in all basic body movements and techniques. This understanding must be demonstrated in the application of techniques under varied circumstances and conditions.

Yondan (4th Dan)

Has excellent knowledge of the principal body movements and techniques and their application under varied conditions to such a degree that the ability to instruct others has been gained.

Godan (5th Dan)

Research has been completed in some limited area.

This research includes its application in a manner that is both relevant and applicable to the individual's particular physique.

Rokudan (6th Dan)

Has completed research in an area that by nature has a universal benefit to be derived by its application.

Shichidan (7th Dan)

Must have undertaken advanced research through actual application and extensive testing of the general research technique.

Hachidan (8th Dan)

Research completed in a new and previously unknown area.

Kudan (9th Dan)

This level calls for an extended period of time to the areas of individual achievement, research and technique. This dedication must have culminated in karate achievement and development of the highest and most extraordinary order. Moreover, this accumulated knowledge and expertise must have been utilized in the general service of karate-do development.

Remember! The Tiger
watches without being seen.

Index